Reading
Between
the Lines

Discovering Christ in the Old Testament

Reading
Between
the Lines
Discovering Christ in the Old Testament

Daniel L. Segraves

WAP ACADEMIC
A Division of Word Aflame Press
8855 Dunn Road, Hazelwood, MO 63042
www.pentecostalpublishing.com

Reading Between the Lines

by Daniel L. Segraves

WAP ACADEMIC
A Division of Word Aflame Press
8855 Dunn Road, Hazelwood, MO 63042
www.pentecostalpublishing.com

Library of Congress Cataloging-in-Publication Data

Contents

Preface

This book has its origin in a series of lessons I wrote and recorded for broadcast on the radio program "Hope University," sponsored by the Media Missions Division of the United Pentecostal Church International. The purpose for the series was to explore the messianic content of the Old Testament, with the idea that this would not only demonstrate the validity of the use made of the Hebrew Scriptures in the New Testament, but that it could also lead to the discovery of details about the life and works of Jesus that may not be seen in the New Testament. In other words, the idea was that to discover what the Old Testament has to say about Jesus can help us know Him even more intimately.

For many years I have been keenly interested in the use of the Old Testament in the New Testament. Hermeneutics is one of my favorite areas of interest, and it seems obvious to me that we can learn something about hermeneutics from those who wrote the New Testament. Much of their work had to do with interpreting the Hebrew Scriptures. They were practicing hermeneutics, but they were doing it under the inspiration of the Holy Spirit. Surely they can be an example to us. Although we are not inspired in the same way they were, we have to believe that the Holy Spirit guided them in such a way that the end result was accurate interpretation of the Law, the Prophets, and the Psalms. Since their understanding of the Old Testament was overwhelmingly messianic, we should also read the Hebrew Scriptures with the Messiah in view.

I would like to express my thanks to Norman R. Paslay II for inviting me to do this series for broadcast. I would also like to thank John Smelser for his ongoing encouragement and affirmation as the project developed. It was a privilege to be involved in the Media Missions ministry.

Daniel L. Segraves

Introduction

Growing in the Knowledge of Our Lord and Savior Jesus Christ

To say we are going to "read between the lines" of Scripture does not mean that we intend to read meaning into the text that is not there. It means we intend to read the Hebrew Scriptures more closely than we may have read them in the past, taking careful note not only of how the Old Testament is used in the New Testament, but also of how those who prophesied and wrote later in the history of Israel understood the texts that had been written earlier. In some cases, we even want to be alert to the way ideas and themes introduced early in a specific book may be further developed or interpreted later within the same book. To do this we must develop a high level of awareness and sensitivity to clues that point back to earlier texts.

It is an adage that the Bible interprets itself. Some theological wag once noted that the Bible throws a lot of light on the commentaries! There is truth in this statement. It has often been said that all translation is interpretation. It could also be said that all writing is interpretation. When the writers of the Old Testament recorded the historical events that happened both before and after the call of Abraham, they were not just preserving the bare bones of history. They were intentionally interpreting that history under the inspiration of the Holy Spirit. As we will see in this book, their interpretation of history resulted in the history itself becoming a prophetic anticipation of future events.

First, we will explore the possibility of coming to know our Lord and Savior Jesus Christ more intimately from the messianic witness of the Old Testament. Then, we will take six chapters to discuss key messianic texts in the Hebrew Scriptures. Four chapters will be occupied with a similar discussion of texts in the Prophets. The following four chapters will do likewise with the Psalms. Finally, in the last chapter, we will comment on the validity of this approach to interpreting Scripture.

No claim is made here to an exhaustive treatment of the messianic witness of the Old Testament. The texts we will explore are merely representative, but they will demonstrate the possibilities that await those who read the Hebrew Scriptures from the same perspective as they were read by those who wrote the New Testament.

When we are finished, I am quite sure we will agree with Peter, who said to the believing Gentiles at the house of Cornelius, "To Him all the prophets witness that, through His name, whoever believes in Him will receive remission of sins" (Acts 10:43). The Holy Spirit gave immediate approval to Peter's assessment of the prophets' testimony to Christ: "While Peter was still speaking these words, the Holy Spirit fell upon all those who heard the word" (Acts 10:44).

Peter, whose initial message on the Day of Pentecost consisted almost exclusively of quotes from the Old Testament with the claim that the Scriptures he quoted were fulfilled by the person and work of Jesus Christ and by the events of that day, understood that at the heart of the Hebrew Scriptures was the anticipation of the Messiah. When Peter proclaimed this on the Day of Pentecost, the result was that three thousand people were added to the church that day. When he proclaimed this at Cornelius's house, the result was qualitatively, if not quantitatively, the same. The Gentiles received the Holy Spirit, speaking with tongues and magnifying God. Then, just as on the Day of Pentecost, Peter commanded them to be baptized in the name of the Lord. (See Acts 10:44-48.)

First-century Christians read the Hebrew Scriptures as if they belonged to the church, as if they witnessed to Christ, and as if they offered specific direction for living the Christian life. They were right to do this. When the New Testament began to be written, the Holy Spirit inspired those who wrote to interpret the Old Testament in the same way.

As we read the Old Testament as did our first-century forebears, we will discover, as they did, that we can come to know our Lord and Savior Jesus Christ more intimately from those pages written so long ago by our ancestors in the faith, those ancient Hebrew prophetic voices.

At the conclusion of his second letter, the apostle Peter encouraged his readers to grow in grace and in the knowledge of our Lord and Savior Jesus Christ.[1] There are various ways this can be done, including prayers when we not only talk with our Lord, but when we also listen for His voice. We can also fellowship with Him in the power of His Holy Spirit. But another way we can grow in the knowledge of Jesus Christ is to explore the rich messianic content of the Hebrew Bible.

For nearly the first fifteen years of its existence, the only Scripture the New Testament church possessed was what we now call the Old Testament. But from this ancient text, those who had put their faith in Jesus Christ were able to proclaim the gospel message and live the Christian life in such an effective way that, in the words of their critics, they turned the world upside down.[2] How could this be done without a New Testament?

The Hebrew Scriptures Testify of Jesus

Shortly after the resurrection of Jesus, two of His disciples were traveling to Emmaus, which was seven miles from Jerusalem. As they discussed the events of the past few days, Jesus drew near and walked along with them. When they did not recognize Him, Jesus asked, "What kind of conversation is this that you have with one another as you walk and are sad?" (Luke 24:17). One of them, Cleopas, answered, "Are You the only stranger in Jerusalem, and have You not known the things which happened there in these days?" (Luke 24:18). Jesus responded, "What things?" (Luke 24:19). "The things concerning Jesus of Nazareth," they replied, "who was a Prophet mighty in deed and word before God and all the people, and how the chief priests and our rulers delivered Him to be condemned to death, and crucified Him" (Luke 24:19-20). The disciples, unaware that they were talking to Jesus, continued, "But we were hoping that it was He who was going to redeem Israel. Indeed, besides all this, today is the third day since these things happened" (Luke 24:21). Then these grieving disciples told Jesus about the empty tomb: "Yes, and certain women of our company, who arrived at the tomb early, astonished us. When they did not find His body, they came saying that they had also seen a vision of angels who said He was alive. And certain of those who were with us went to the tomb and found it just as the women had said; but Him they did not see" (Luke 24:22-24).

How do you suppose Jesus responded to these disciples that day on the road to Emmaus? Would He express sympathy for them? Would He say, "I know how you feel. How could you possibly know that these things would happen to the Messiah?" No, that was not His response. Instead, Jesus said, "O foolish ones, and slow of heart to believe in all that the prophets have spoken! Ought not the Christ to have suffered these things and to enter into His glory?" (Luke 24:25-26). The prophets to whom Jesus referred were the Hebrew prophets, those whose words were recorded in what we call the Old Testament. If these disciples had known what the prophets said about the Messiah, they would have understood that all that had happened over the past few days had been foretold centuries before. So, instead of expressing empathy with Cleopas and his friend in their disappointment, Jesus began "at Moses and all the Prophets" and expounded "to them in all the Scriptures the things concerning Himself" (Luke 24:27). To say that Jesus began at Moses means He began at the first of the Hebrew Bible with the books of Genesis, Exodus, Leviticus, Numbers, and Deuteronomy. The reference to the Prophets means that Jesus continued from Moses, which is commonly called the law or the Pentateuch, to the book of Joshua, the first of the prophets, and all of the books following Joshua. In other words, Jesus explained to these two disciples what the Old Testament, from its very beginning, had to say about Him.

Later, when Jesus vanished from the sight of the disciples as they were sharing a meal, they said to one another, "Did not our heart burn within us while He talked with us on the road, and while He opened the Scriptures to us?" (Luke 24:32). These disciples understood the Hebrew Scriptures only when Jesus explained the Scriptures in terms of what they said about Him. Cleopas and his friend wasted no time in returning to Jerusalem to share with the eleven disciples what they had experienced.[3]

As the gathered disciples talked about the resurrection of Jesus, Jesus Himself suddenly stood among them, saying, "Peace to you" (Luke 24:36). But even though the disciples knew Christ had risen, they reacted with terror and fear. They thought they had seen a ghost.[4] So Jesus said, "Why are you troubled? And why do doubts arise in your hearts? Behold My hands and My feet, that it is I Myself. Handle Me and see, for a spirit does not have flesh and bones as you see I have" (Luke 24:38-39). Although Jesus showed them His hands and feet, the disciples were so overcome with joy and wonder they still could not believe what they were seeing. So Jesus asked, "Have you any food here?" (Luke 24:41). Then they gave Jesus a piece of fish and part of a honeycomb, which He ate in their presence.[5]

Then, opening their understanding and enabling His disciples to comprehend the Scriptures, Jesus said, "These are the words which I spoke to you while I was still with you, that all things must be fulfilled which were written in the Law of Moses and the Prophets and the Psalms concerning Me. Thus it is written, and thus it was necessary for the Christ to suffer and to rise from the dead the third day, and that repentance and remission of sins should be preached in His name to all nations, beginning at Jerusalem" (Luke 24:44, 46-47). He continued, "And you are witnesses of these things. Behold, I send the Promise of My Father upon you; but tarry in the city of Jerusalem until you are endued with power from on high" (Luke 24:48-49).

These words, which Jesus spoke just before He ascended into heaven, have profound implications. They tell us that the essential story of redemption is found in the Old Testament before it is ever found in the New Testament. Indeed, as we will discover, there are details about Christ's life and work recorded in the Old Testament that never found their way into the New Testament. As we explore the pages of the Hebrew Bible, mining the rich veins of messianic truth found there, we will come to know our Lord even better. We will, as Peter exhorted, grow in our knowledge of the Lord and Savior, Jesus Christ.

Did you notice that Jesus said that everything that is written concerning Him in the Law, the Prophets, and the Psalms must be fulfilled? When Jesus used the terms "law," "prophets," and "psalms," He described the entirety of the Old Testament, from the beginning to the end. Although in English translations the order of the books and the division of some of the books are different than in the Hebrew Bible, the content is the same. Therefore, these words of Jesus endorse in full what we know today as the Old Testament. It is a wonderful thing to know that instead of being a dry, uninteresting account of ancient history, the Law, the Prophets, and the Psalms speak of Jesus Christ.

But how specific is the information about Christ found in the Old Testament? We will discover it is quite specific, right down to minute details. Notice that Jesus told His disciples the following things are written in the Old Testament. First, the Hebrew Scriptures testify the Messiah would suffer. The events of Christ's betrayal by Judas Iscariot, the suffering of Christ on the Cross, the mockery of the unbelieving passersby, the dividing of His garments by those who gambled at the foot of the cross, the piercing of His hands and feet, and His death are all foretold in the Old Testament. Even the words of the prayers Jesus prayed while on the cross are found in the Old Testament.

But the Hebrew Bible foretold not only the sufferings of Christ; it also anticipated His resurrection from the dead on the third day. Notice how specific this is. It would have been marvelous if the prophets had foretold only His resurrection, but they went beyond that to declare even the day of His resurrection.

When we take another look at Jesus' final words, we note that in addition to foretelling the suffering and resurrection of Christ, the Old Testament also announced that repentance and remission of sins should be preached in His name to all nations, beginning at Jerusalem. It should be no surprise that Jesus commanded His disciples to wait in the city of Jerusalem for the promise of the Father, the gift of the Holy Spirit.[6] In many places the Old Testament connects salvation with Zion, or Jerusalem. For example, Isaiah wrote, "I bring My righteousness near, it shall not be far off; my salvation shall not linger. And I will place salvation in Zion, for Israel My glory" (Isaiah 46:13). Joel prophesied, "And it shall come to pass that whoever calls on the name of the LORD shall be saved. For in Mount Zion and in Jerusalem there shall be deliverance, as the LORD has said, among the remnant whom the LORD calls" (Joel 2:32). Zechariah wrote, "Rejoice greatly, O daughter of Zion! Shout, O daughter of Jerusalem! Behold, your King is coming to you; He is just and having salvation, lowly and riding on a donkey, a colt, the foal of a donkey" (Zechariah 9:9). In conjunction with Jesus' entrance into Jerusalem, Matthew wrote, "All this was done that it might be fulfilled which was spoken by the prophet, saying: 'Tell the daughter of Zion, "Behold, your King is coming to you, lowly, and sitting on a donkey, a colt, the foal of a donkey"'" (Matthew 21:4-5).

The Hebrew Scriptures Anticipate Pentecost

Neither should it be a surprise to us, in view of the anticipation of these events in the Old Testament, that after the Holy Spirit was poured out on the waiting believers in Jerusalem, the apostle Peter connected the events of that day with the promises made by the Hebrew prophets. Jesus said it was written that repentance and remission of sins should be preached in His name to all nations, beginning at Jerusalem. After those who observed the miracle of Holy Spirit baptism on the Day of Pentecost asked, "What shall we do?" (Acts 2:37), Peter, in fulfillment of Old Testament prophecy and in harmony with Jesus' last words, said, "Repent, and let every one of you be baptized in the name of Jesus Christ for the remission of sins; and you shall receive the gift of the

Holy Spirit" (Acts 2:38). As Jesus had said, connecting these events with the Hebrew prophets, repentance and remission of sins were now being preached in His name, beginning in Jerusalem. And, as Jesus also declared, this message would soon spread to all nations.

Neither Cleopas and his friend on the road to Emmaus nor the rest of the disciples fully understood the Hebrew Scriptures until Jesus explained that the Law, the Prophets, and the Psalms spoke of Him. Once their eyes were opened to the messianic content of the Old Testament, the disciples went everywhere, preaching the gospel of Jesus Christ from the same book that we now call the Old Testament. Even the apostle Paul, who did not believe on Christ until after the establishment of the church, reasoned from the Scriptures—meaning the Hebrew Scriptures, "explaining and demonstrating that the Christ had to suffer and rise again from the dead, and saying, 'This Jesus whom I preached to you is the Christ,'" or the Messiah (Acts 17:2-3). The fair-minded Jews of Berea "received the word with all readiness, and searched the Scriptures daily to find out whether these things were so" (Acts 17:11). The Scriptures they searched are those found in our Old Testament today. After the husband and wife ministry team, Aquila and Priscilla, explained the Hebrew Scriptures more accurately to Apollos, this powerful preacher was vigorous in "showing from the Scriptures that Jesus is the Christ" (Acts 18:28). When Paul was accused of heresy, he said, "I worship the God of my fathers, believing all things which are written in the Law and in the Prophets" (Acts 24:14). As he awaited judgment in Rome, Paul "explained and solemnly testified of the kingdom of God, persuading" his hearers "concerning Jesus from both the Law of

Moses and the Prophets, from morning till evening" (Acts 28:23).

Paul's Use of the Hebrew Scriptures

Paul's ministry, from the very beginning, was rich in the use of the Hebrew Scriptures to proclaim Christ as the promised Messiah and the work being done by Christ in the church as the fulfillment of Hebrew prophecy. Paul rooted his teaching exclusively in the Scriptures.

When he was called before Agrippa, Paul said it was "for the hope of the promise made by God to [the] fathers" (Acts 26:6). In a clear appeal to the Hebrew Scriptures for his message, Paul told Agrippa that he said nothing other than those things "which the prophets and Moses said would come—that the Christ would suffer, that He would be the first to rise from the dead, and would proclaim light to the Jewish people and to the Gentiles" (Acts 26:22-23). Rather than claiming innovation for his message, Paul insisted that he said nothing new.[7] After arriving in Rome, Paul told the Jewish community there he had done nothing against the Jewish people or the fathers (Acts 28:17). Instead, he was bound "for the hope of Israel" (Acts 28:20).

When he wrote to the believers at Rome, Paul declared the gospel of God was that "which he promised before through His prophets in the Holy Scriptures" (Romans 1:1-2). The Law and the Prophets witness to the righteousness of God through faith in Jesus Christ "to all and on all who believe. For there is no difference" (Romans 3:21-22). As he concluded the letter, Paul wrote that the gospel he preached was made known to all nations "by the prophetic Scriptures" (Romans 16:25-26). This can only mean the message he preached in the churches was firmly rooted in the Old Testament.

In his first letter to the Corinthians Paul explained he spoke "the wisdom of God in a mystery, the hidden wisdom which God ordained before the ages" (I Corinthians 2:7). But this mystery was anticipated in the Hebrew Scriptures (I Corinthians 2:9). It had now been revealed to Paul "through His Spirit. For the Spirit searches all things, yes, the deep things of God" (I Corinthians 2:10). In a clear explanation of the essential gospel message, Paul wrote, "For I delivered to you first of all that which I also received: that Christ died for our sins according to the Scriptures, and that He was buried, and that He rose again the third day according to the Scriptures" (I Corinthians 15:3-4). When Paul said "according to the Scriptures," he was referring to what we know as the Old Testament. So not only does the Old Testament foretell the suffering and death of the Messiah; it also informs us His death was "for our sins." The meaning of the Greek word translated "gospel" is "good news." The gospel is good news because it tells us that since Jesus died for our sins, we no longer have a sin problem if we are willing to receive the benefits of His work on our behalf. And, as Jesus said just before He ascended, Paul reported that the resurrection of Jesus on the third day was "according to the Scriptures."

In his second letter to the Corinthians Paul explained that those who read the Hebrew Scriptures while rejecting Christ are hindered by a veil; their minds are blinded (II Corinthians 3:14).

In his letter to the believers in Galatia Paul declared the Hebrew Scriptures "preached the gospel to Abraham beforehand" (Galatians 3:8b). In receiving "the blessing of Abraham," Gentiles are also receiving "the promise of the Spirit through faith" (Galatians 3:14). When "the Scripture ... confine[s] all under sin," Gentiles are included along with Jews, so "that the promise by faith in Jesus Christ might be given to those who believe" (Galatians 3:22).

To the Ephesians Paul quoted Psalm 68:18 to explain the gifts of apostles, prophets, evangelists, pastors, and teachers to the church (Ephesians 4:7-14).

In his letter to the Colossians, Paul saw the regulations concerning food, drink, festivals, new moons, and sabbaths—all integral to the law of Moses—as being "shadow[s] of things to come, but the substance is of Christ" (Colossians 2:16-17).

In his second letter to Timothy, Paul declared the Holy Scriptures—the inspired Hebrew Scriptures that Timothy had known from childhood—"are able to make you wise for salvation through faith which is in Christ Jesus" (II Timothy 3:15). It is precisely these Scriptures that are "profitable for doctrine, for reproof, for correction, for instruction in righteousness, that the man of God may be complete, thoroughly equipped for every good work" (II Timothy 3:16-17). The Hebrew Scriptures are profitable for church doctrine, for the reproof, correction, and instruction of church members, and they are capable of bringing a man of God who is in the church to completion.

The Old Testament is truly a Christ-centered book.

Marcion's Mistake

In the second century AD, Marcion rejected the entirety of the Old Testament. He claimed it was the work of an inferior God of justice, but that Jesus Christ was the messenger of another God, the supreme and good

God. Since the New Testament so frequently refers to the Old Testament, Marcion also found it necessary to reject most of the New Testament as well. He was left with eleven books, Luke and ten of Paul's letters. But before he could accept even these, Marcion had to purge them of all references to the Old Testament.

Marcion was wrong, of course. The Old Testament is consumed with the promise of the good news of the gospel in Christ Jesus. The New Testament quotes, paraphrases, or alludes to the Old Testament nearly eight hundred times. By doing so, the New Testament connects with the message of the Old Testament, where the coming of the Messiah and His redemptive work are foretold. As John wrote, just before the close of the New Testament, "The testimony of Jesus is the spirit of prophecy" (Revelation 19:10).

In the following chapters, we will explore the Old Testament's testimony of the Messiah, Jesus. As we do, we will come to know our Lord more fully from the pages of the Law, the Prophets, and the Psalms. We will follow the example of our first-century spiritual ancestors and read the Hebrew Scriptures from the perspective of their witness to our Lord and Savior, Jesus Christ.

Part I

How the Law Reveals Jesus

1

In the Beginning

In order to discover what the Old Testament—the Hebrew Scripture—has to say about Jesus, we must learn to be alert to references to the Old Testament as they are found in the New Testament. Phrases like "as it is written" or references to the prophets are the kinds of clues for which we should look. Many study Bibles are helpful because they set off quotes from the Old Testament in a different typeface, with indents, or by some other visual indication. Although these techniques are useful, we should not rely on them to give us an exhaustive list of the references to the Old Testament in the New Testament, because the nearly eight hundred references to the Hebrew Bible in the New Testament are not always in the form of complete quotes. These references include paraphrases and allusions, which may not be indicated by typical introductory language such as "it is written" or by typographical techniques. To be sure we are aware of every use the New Testament makes of the Old Testament, there is no substitute for simply reading the text carefully.

Innertextuality and Intertextuality

If we wish to explore the messianic content of the Old Testament, it is important we be aware of something called innertextuality and intertextuality.[8] These terms refer to the use Scripture makes of Scripture. We have discussed the use of the Old Testament in the New Testament. This is intertextuality. In other words, intertextuality has to do with how those who wrote Scripture quoted or referred to other Scriptures that had already been written. Often intertextuality helps us interpret Scripture. The way later authors referred to earlier authors is interpretive. For example, on the Day of Pentecost, after the Holy Spirit was poured out on the waiting believers, and in response to the question, "Whatever could this mean?" (Acts 2:12), Peter answered, "This is what was spoken by the prophet Joel" (Acts 2:16). Then Peter quoted Joel 2:28-32, indicating that Joel had anticipated the events of the Day of Pentecost. Then, as recorded in Acts 2:25-28, Peter quoted from Psalm 16:8-11 to declare that David wrote of Jesus Christ. These are examples of a form of intertextuality.

But there is also innertextuality, which refers to a biblical author referring back to something already written in an earlier part of the same book. For example, Psalm 1, which is part of the introduction to the Book of Psalms, describes a contrast between the righteous and the wicked. This contrast forms a major part of the structure of the Psalter, and it is referred to again and again in the following psalms. Each time there is a reference to the righteous and the wicked, it is rooted in Psalm 1, further explaining and developing the contrast between the two.

For our purposes, we want to look at an example of intertextuality in the Bible. When we do this, it is important to read the Bible carefully, being alert to the appearance of phrases that are similar to phrases that appear elsewhere in Scripture. Since Jesus opened the Scripture to the two disciples on the road to Emmaus by starting with the first book of the Bible, let's do the same.

In the Beginning

The first verse of the Bible, Genesis 1:1, reads, "In the beginning God created the heavens and the earth." The phrase "in the beginning" immediately reminds us of another place in the Bible where these same words appear. The apostle John wrote, "In the beginning was the Word, and the Word was with God, and the Word was God. The same was in the beginning with God" (John 1:1-2, KJV). Not only did John twice use the phrase "in the beginning"—the same phrase that appears in the first verse of the Bible, but he was also discussing the same subject: Creation. John wrote, "All things were made by him; and without him was not anything made that was made" (John 1:3, KJV).

But this is not the only time John referred to the beginning. In the opening verses of his first letter, just as in the Gospel of John 1:1-2, John wrote of the beginning: "That which was from the beginning, which we have heard, which we have seen with our eyes, which we have looked upon, and our hands have handled, concerning the Word of life—the life was manifested, and we have seen, and bear witness, and declare to you that eternal life which was with the Father and was manifested to us." The similarities between John 1:1-2 and I John 1:1-2 are remarkable. In both places, John referred to the beginning and to the Word. And there is a further connection between these two texts: In John 1:14, John wrote that "the Word became flesh and dwelt among us, and we beheld His glory, the glory as of the only begotten of the Father, full of grace and truth." This is, of course, a reference to Jesus Christ, the Word made flesh. In his first letter, John discussed the same subject in similar words: "the life was manifested, and we have seen, and bear witness, and declare to you that eternal life which was with the Father and was manifested to us" (I John 1:2). In his Gospel, John wrote that the Word became flesh; in his first letter, he wrote that the Word of life was manifested in such a way as to be seen and handled. This is certainly an example of intertextuality, and we will look at it again to see what it tells us about Jesus.

But we should note that there is yet another use of the phrase "in the beginning" in the New Testament with an apparent connection with Genesis 1:1. In Hebrews 1, several verses are quoted from the Old Testament to show that Jesus is superior to the angels. These references include Psalm 2:7, II Samuel 7:14, Deuteronomy 32:43, Psalm 104:4, and Psalm 45:6-7. Then, in Hebrews 1:10-12, we find a quote from the Old Testament that uses the phrase "in the beginning" in a reference to creation, just as in Genesis 1:1. It reads, "And: You LORD, in the beginning laid the foundation of the earth, and the heavens are the work of Your hands. They will perish, but You remain; and they will all grow old like a garment; like a cloak You will fold them up, and they will be changed. But You are the same, and Your years will not fail." This quote from Psalm 102:25-27 is quite interesting because it is a reference in the New Testament to a Scripture in the Old Testament that is itself a reference to an earlier Scripture. This is certainly an excellent example of intertextuality.

How do these Scriptures help us know Jesus more fully? When we examine them carefully, we can see that the New Testament references to Genesis 1:1 serve to identify Jesus Christ as the God who created the heavens and the earth. The word translated "God" in Genesis 1:1 is the Hebrew, *Elohim.* Although this word is plural in form, it is singular in reference. In the Hebrew language, plural words are used not only to indicate more than one of something, but also to indicate intensity or fullness of a singular referent. One way we determine whether the noun *Elohim* refers to a singular or plural referent is to note whether the verb used with this noun is singular or plural. In the Hebrew language, singular nouns have singular verbs, and plural nouns ordinarily have plural verbs. But if a plural noun is accompanied by a singular verb, the noun must be read as singular. In Genesis 1:1, the plural *Elohim*, translated "God," has a singular verb, *bara'*, translated "created." Therefore, we know that the God who created the heavens and the earth was one singular God. This should be kept in mind when we read the references to Genesis 1:1 that are found in the New Testament. If the first mention to the work of creation in the beginning indicates that the God who did the creative work is one, we should expect further references to this event to agree with this idea. In other words, we should not expect to discover later in Scripture that more than one God was involved in the work of creation.

In the Beginning Was the Word

When we come to John's reference to the beginning and to creation in the Gospel of John, we seek to understand John in terms of Genesis 1:1. Although intertextuality suggests that later references to earlier Scriptures will serve an interpretive purpose, these later references will not function in such a way as to contradict or to conflict with earlier Scriptures. John wrote, "In the beginning was the Word, and the Word was with God, and the Word was God." The Greek word translated "word" is *logos*. What did John mean by "word" or *logos*? *Logos* was a term commonly used by ancient Greek philosophers. To them, *logos* referred to reason as the controlling principle of the universe. They did not, however, believe that *logos* or reason was God. Is this what John meant by his use of "word"? No, for John sees the Word as a reference to the God who created all things. It is much more likely that John was writing from the perspective of the Aramaic Targums than that he was writing from the perspective of Greek philosophy.

Aramaic is a cognate language with Hebrew, that is to say that Aramaic is related to Hebrew. In the first century AD in Israel, Aramaic was the common conversational language. We know Jesus spoke Aramaic, for there are places in the Gospels where his Aramaic words are recorded, then translated into Greek for non-Jewish readers who would not have been familiar with Aramaic. For example, in Mark 5:41, Jesus is quoted as saying, *Talitha cumi*. This is Aramaic for "little girl, arise." Since Aramaic was the conversational language among the Jewish people of the first century, the Hebrew Scriptures were translated or paraphrased into Aramaic so they could be read. These translations are known as the Targums. John would have been familiar with them.

In the Targums, the Aramaic word *memra*, which means "word," is often used to designate God in activity. Bruce Metzger pointed out that "reverence for the God of Israel led the Targumist to employ surrogates for the Deity, such as 'Word' (*Memra*)."[9] For example, in Genesis 1:16-17, where the English translation reads, "Then God made two great lights," one Targum reads, "The Word of the Lord created the two large luminaries," and where Genesis 2:2 reads, "And on the seventh day God ended His work which He had done," the Targum reads, "On the seventh day the Word of the Lord completed the work which he had created."[10]

But it is not just the Targums that identify God with His Word. So do the Hebrew Scriptures. For example, Psalm 33:6 reads, "By the word of the LORD the heavens were made, and all the host of them by the breath of His mouth." The striking poetry of Psalm 29:3-5, 8 identifies God with His voice: "The voice of the LORD is over the waters; the God of glory thunders; the LORD is over many waters. The voice of the LORD is powerful; the voice of the LORD is full of majesty. The voice of the LORD breaks the cedars, Yes, the LORD splinters the cedars of Lebanon ... The voice of the LORD shakes the wilderness; the LORD shakes the Wilderness of Kadesh." The parallelism of Hebrew poetry means that the voice of the LORD is none other than the LORD Himself. The voice of the LORD cannot be distinguished from the LORD Himself.

It was against this background that John wrote, "In the beginning was the Word, and the Word was with God, and the Word was God. The same was in the beginning with God" (John 1:1-2). John did not mean that reason was in the beginning, that reason was with God, and that reason was God. Nor did John mean that reason created all things. Instead, he wrote that all things were made by the Word and that nothing that was made was made apart from the Word (John 1:3). It is quite clear, as John indicated in the first verse of his Gospel, that the Word was God. But in its intertextual function with Genesis 1:1, John 1 identifies the God who created all things as none other than the one we know as Jesus Christ! John wrote, "And the Word became flesh and dwelt among us, and we beheld His glory, the glory as of the only begotten of the Father, full of grace and truth" (John 1:14).

The Error of Docetism

But the question immediately arises: If the Word is *with* God, as indicated in John 1:1, and if the Word is *the only begotten of the Father*, as seen in John 1:14, how can the Word at the same time *be* God? It is at precisely this point that the intertextual interpretation seen in John's first epistle brings great clarity. Apparently John wrote his first letter at least in part as a response to docetism, an early heresy that denied the genuineness of Christ's humanity. The word "docetism" comes from the Greek *dokē* , meaning "to seem." Docetists claimed that Jesus merely seemed to be human; his humanity was like a mirage; it was merely an appearance of human existence. In their view, if you had attempted to pat Jesus on the back, your hand would have passed right through Him. Thus, His suffering and death on the cross were not real; He merely seemed to suffer and die. John resisted this false teaching with strong words. He wrote, "Beloved, do not believe every spirit, but test the spirits, whether they are of God; because many false prophets have gone out into the world. By this you know the Spirit of God: Every spirit that confesses that Jesus Christ has come in the flesh is of God, and every spirit that does not confess that Jesus Christ has come in the flesh is not of God. And this is the spirit of the Antichrist, which you have heard was coming, and is now already in the world" (I John 4:1-3). To believe in the genuineness of Christ's humanity is not an option; to deny it is to deny the Incarnation.

The Word of Life

But John did not wait to confront docetism until the fourth chapter of his letter. He exposed this error in the opening of the book. He wrote, "We have heard ... we have seen with our eyes ... we have looked upon, and our hands have handled ... the Word of life" (I John 1:1). This Word of Life was "from the beginning." Jesus was no phantom; the apostles had not only seen Him, they had also touched Him with their hands. Here John's subject was the same as in the Gospel of John: the beginning and the Word, or the *logos*. Here, however, I John helps us understand what is meant by Word (*logos*) in the Gospel of John. I John identifies the Word as the "Word of life." Whereas in his Gospel John wrote that the Word became flesh, in his first letter he wrote that "the life was manifested." And what life was this? It was, John said, "that eternal life which was with the Father and was manifested to us" (I John 1:2). In his Gospel, John wrote that the Word was with God; in his first letter, he wrote that eternal life, which he previously identified as the Word of Life, was with the Father. It was this eternal life, this Word of Life, which was manifested to us in the person of Jesus Christ.

By the inspired genius of its intertextuality, the Bible informs us that the God who created the heavens and the earth in the beginning is none other than the God we know in His manifestation in the flesh as Jesus

Christ. He is not a God distinct from the Creator; He is the Creator Himself. He can no more be distinguished from the Creator than one's life can be distinguished from oneself. He is the eternal life that was with the Father and was manifested to us.

Jesus is Yahweh

The final example of intertextuality relating to Genesis 1:1 underscores this idea. In Hebrews 1:10, we find these words: "And: You LORD, in the beginning laid the foundation of the earth, and the heavens are the work of Your hands." As we examine the context, the first thing we notice about this Scripture is that these words are spoken to the Son, our Lord Jesus Christ. Hebrews 1:8-9 read, "But to the Son He says: 'Your throne, O God, is forever and ever; a scepter of righteousness is the scepter of Your kingdom. You have loved righteousness and hated lawlessness; therefore God, Your God, has anointed You with the oil of gladness more than Your companions.'" Hebrews 1:10 begins with the word "and," connecting the words to follow with the previous words, continuing with that which was spoken to the Son. Hebrews 1:8, which identifies the Son as God by means of a quote from Psalm 45:6, indicates the deity of Jesus; Hebrews 1:9, which identifies the Son as the Messiah by virtue of His anointing, indicates the humanity of Jesus. It is only in His humanity that Jesus has "companions," or peers. But then, in Hebrews 1:10, the Son is identified as Yahweh, the covenant name by which God revealed Himself to Moses in Exodus 6:3. Most English translations indicate the Hebrew behind the English words used to represent the name of God by typographical conventions. Specifically, when the Hebrew

34

word is Yahweh, most translations will represent this by the word LORD, with all capital letters. Some English translations expand this convention into the New Testament by capitalizing the word LORD when the New Testament quotes an Old Testament text where the word Yahweh appears. Such is the case with Hebrews 1:10, which is quoted from the Greek Septuagint translation of Psalm 102:25. Since it is Yahweh who is addressed in Psalm 102, as indicated in verse 1, the Septuagint translates verse 25 as, "In the beginning thou, O Lord, didst lay the foundation of the earth; and the heavens are the works of thine hands." Thus, the writer of Hebrews identifies the Son as Yahweh, the Creator. By its connection with Psalm 102, and by the connection of Psalm 102 with Genesis 1:1, the Book of Hebrews, like the Gospel of John and the letter of I John, informs us that the singular God who created the heavens and the earth is none other than Jesus Christ. He is the Word, the Word of Life, the very life of the Father, manifested in genuine, authentic human existence.

It would be impossible to describe the miraculous mystery of the Incarnation more fittingly than in Paul's words in I Timothy 3:16: "And without controversy great is the mystery of godliness: God was manifested in the flesh, justified in the Spirit, seen by angels, preached among the Gentiles, believed on in the world, received up in glory." In knowing Jesus, we know the Creator Himself. This wondrous truth is rooted in the very first verse of the Bible.

2

An Early Prophecy
of the Messiah

It has long been recognized by students of the Bible that one of the earliest prophecies of the coming Messiah is found in Genesis 3:15. After the serpent successfully tempted Eve in the Garden of Eden, leading to Adam's downfall as well, the LORD God said to the serpent, "Because you have done this, you are cursed more than all cattle, and more than every beast of the field; on your belly you shall go, and you shall eat dust all the days of your life. And I will put enmity between you and the woman, and between your seed and her Seed; He shall bruise your head, and you shall bruise His heel" (Genesis 3:14-15). In chapter 2, we noted the importance of innertextuality and intertextuality in interpreting Scripture. Intertextuality has to do with the way later Scripture refers to earlier Scripture. Innertextuality has to do with the way a specific book of the Bible makes use of earlier statements found in the same book. Both innertextuality and intertextuality serve an interpretive function. This is, in other words, part of what it means to say that the Bible interprets itself.

As we consider Genesis 3:15, we will see how this early prophecy, which may seem somewhat obscure at first, is referred to in later Scripture in such a way as to make it quite clear that the prophecy is about the Messiah and His victory over Satan.

A Prophecy in Three Parts

Let's look closely at the prophecy itself. It consists of three parts. First, the LORD said to the serpent, "I will put enmity between you and the woman." Second, He said, "And between your seed and her Seed." Third, He concluded, "He shall bruise your head, and you shall bruise His heel." The first part of the prophecy refers to the fact that from that time forward, there would be enmity between a human being, Eve, and a member of the animal kingdom, the serpent that had been an instrument of Satan to tempt her. This enmity did not exist previously, which explains why Eve was willing to talk with the serpent. From this time forward, Eve would consider the serpent to be her enemy.

Second, the LORD said to the serpent that He would put enmity between the serpent's seed and Eve's seed. The Hebrew word *zera`*, translated "seed," has a range of meaning. In this context, it refers first to the offspring of the serpent and then to the offspring of Eve. The point is that the enmity introduced between the serpent and Eve would be expanded to include their descendants. Following the flood of Noah, this enmity was further expanded to include the entire animal kingdom. To Noah, God said, "And the fear of you and the dread of you shall be on every beast of the earth, on every bird of the air, on all that move on the earth, and on all the fish of the sea. They are given into your hand" (Genesis 9:2). The enmity between humans and animals is a consequence of sin that will one day be removed, as can be seen in Isaiah 11:6-9: "The wolf also shall dwell with the lamb, the leopard shall lie down with the young goat, the calf and the young lion and the fatling together; and a little child shall lead them. The cow and the bear shall graze; their young ones shall lie down together; and the lion shall eat straw like the ox. The nursing child shall play by the cobra's hole, and the weaned child shall put his hand in the viper's den. They shall not hurt nor destroy in all My holy mountain, for the earth shall be full of the knowledge of the LORD as the waters cover the sea." This describes the era of the millennium, and the reversal of enmity is due to the Messiah's redemptive work, as may be seen in Isaiah 11:1-5, 10. But before the fall of humans into sin, as recorded in Genesis 3, there was peace between humans and animals. This can be seen in the fact that all creatures were brought before Adam so that he could name them.[11] In biblical thought, to name something or someone is associated with having authority over that thing or person. But as a result of sin, this peace was destroyed, and there is tension between humans and animals to this day.

The third part of the curse on the serpent is specifically messianic. The LORD said, "He shall bruise your head, and you shall bruise His heel." At this point, the focus shifts from the enmity between the serpent and Eve and from the serpent's descendants and Eve's descendants to the enmity between a specific male descendant of Eve and the serpent himself. This is a long view that extends beyond the lifetime of Eve and the lifetime of the physical serpent that was used of Satan to tempt her; thus, the "you" in view in the phrase "you shall bruise His heel" does not refer to the physical serpent in Eden, which would be dead long before this prophecy was fulfilled, but to Satan, the spiritual entity that made use of the physical serpent. This will be seen as we look at the intertextual use made of this prophecy elsewhere in Scripture. Before we leave this prophecy, however, we should note that the enmity between the serpent and the male descendant of Eve would result in death for both. But the death of Eve's descendant, the Messiah, is pictured in such a way as to indicate, even in death, His superiority over the serpent, Satan: Although the serpent would bruise the Messiah's heel, the Messiah would bruise the serpent's head. It would be in the very act of bruising the serpent's head that the Messiah's heel would be bruised.

The Seed of the Woman

Many years later, the Messiah came; our Lord Jesus Christ was a descendant of Eve. Paul pointed out that "when the fullness of the time had come, God sent forth His Son, born of a woman, born under the law" (Galatians 4:4). This reflects the announcement of the angel Gabriel to Mary, the mother of Jesus. Gabriel said, "Rejoice, highly favored one, the Lord is with you: blessed are you among women!" (Luke 1:28). Mary was troubled at this, but Gabriel continued, "Do not be afraid, Mary, for you have found favor with God. And behold, you will conceive in your womb and bring forth a Son, and shall call His name JESUS" (Luke 1:30-31). In Luke's account of the genealogy of Jesus, the ancestors of Jesus are traced all the way back to Adam.[12] Since Jesus was a descendant of

Adam, He was, of course, a descendant of Eve. The name "Eve" means "life" or "living." The reason Adam named his wife Eve is "because she was the mother of all living" (Genesis 3:20).

The Temptation of Jesus

After His baptism by John, "Jesus was led up by the Spirit into the wilderness to be tempted by the devil" (Matthew 4:1). In his second temptation, the devil took Jesus up into the holy city and set Him on the pinnacle of the Temple. Then he said to Jesus, "If You are the Son of God, throw Yourself down. For it is written: 'He shall give His angels charge over you,' and 'in their hands they shall bear you up, lest you dash your foot against a stone'" (Matthew 4:6). In this temptation, Satan quoted from Psalm 91:11-12. We should not understand the word "if" to indicate that Satan questioned whether Jesus was the Son of God. In New Testament Greek, a variety of conditional statements are possible, moving from the first class condition that affirms the reality of the condition to the fourth class condition that assumes that the condition is possible in the future.[13] In Matthew 4:6, the first class condition is used. The meaning is, "Since you are the Son of God, throw Yourself down." Satan knew that Jesus was the Son of God, so he quoted from a messianic prophecy in his temptation. Notice that Jesus did not resist Satan by claiming that the promise of Psalm 91 did not pertain to Him. Instead, He quoted yet another Scripture to show that the promises of God must not be treated presumptuously; He replied, "It is written again, 'You shall not tempt the LORD your God'" (Matthew 4:7).

If we keep Genesis 3:15 in mind when we look at Psalm 91, it becomes quite clear that this psalm, like so many others, is about the Messiah. When we read the psalms, we should always remember Jesus said that everything written concerning Him in the psalms must be fulfilled.[14] Notice the context of Psalm 91:11-12: "For He shall give His angels charge over you, to keep you in all your ways. In their hands they shall bear you up, lest you dash your foot against a stone." The next verse reads, "You shall tread upon the lion and the cobra, the young lion and the serpent you shall trample underfoot." Throughout Scripture, Satan is represented as, among other things, a serpent, a dragon, and a lion. For example Psalm 22, the source of the words which Jesus prayed on the cross when He cried out, "My God, My God, why have You forsaken Me?", also includes these words: "The congregation of the wicked has enclosed Me. They pierced My hands and My feet; I can count all My bones. They look and stare at Me. They divide My garments among them. And for My clothing they cast lots. But you, O LORD, do not be far from Me; O My Strength, hasten to help Me! Deliver Me from the sword, My precious life from the power of the dog. Save Me from the lion's mouth and from the horns of the wild oxen!" (Psalm 22:16-21). John described the binding of Satan like this: "Then I saw an angel coming down from heaven, having the key to the bottomless pit and a great chain in his hand. He laid hold of the dragon, that serpent of old, who is the Devil and Satan, and bound him for a thousand years" (Revelation 20:1-2). Peter wrote that believers should be "sober, be vigilant; because your adversary the devil walks about like a roaring lion, seeking whom he may devour" (I Peter 5:8). Paul wrote: "But I fear, lest somehow, as the serpent deceived Eve by his craftiness, so your minds may be corrupted from the simplicity that is in Christ" (II Corinthians 11:3). So when we see, in Psalm 91:13, the promise, "You shall tread upon the lion and the cobra, the young lion and the serpent you shall trample underfoot," we should not think this has to do exclusively with a promise to believers in general that they will have authority over the animal kingdom. Instead, we should notice the connection this promise has with Genesis 3:15—its intertextuality that is apparent by comparing the statement "He shall bruise your head" with the statement "the serpent you shall trample underfoot"—and the way Psalm 91 is used in the New Testament—another example of intertextuality. If Psalm 91 is not a promise to the Messiah, there would have been no point for Satan to quote from it in his attempt to gain a victory over Jesus. It was a temptation precisely because it was a promise to the Messiah, but Jesus resisted the temptation because He recognized Satan's effort to cause Him to abuse this promise by presumptuously taking it for granted. To do this would be to tempt or to test God, and this was forbidden elsewhere in Scripture.[15]

The Death of the Serpent

The prophecy of Genesis 3:15 anticipated the death of the Messiah; the serpent would bruise His heel. But it also foretold the death of the serpent. The Messiah would crush the serpent's head. How would this happen? The answer is alluded to in the prophecy itself; it would be by means of the miracle of the Incarnation—God would be manifest in flesh. In other words, the Seed of the woman, the descendant of Eve, would not only be a human being; He would also be God Himself. This idea is developed in Hebrews 2:14-17: "Inasmuch then as the children have partaken of flesh and blood, He Himself likewise shared in the same, that through death He might destroy him who had the power of death, that is, the devil, and release those who through fear of death were all their lifetime subject to bondage. For indeed He does not give aid to angels, but He does give aid to the seed of Abraham. Therefore, in all things He had to be made like His brethren, that He might be a merciful and faithful High Priest in things pertaining to God, to make propitiation for the sins of the people." Notice again this phrase: that through death He might destroy him who had the power of death, that is, the devil. Although the serpent would bruise His heel, a reference to the Messiah's death, it would be through that very death the Messiah would crush the serpent's head or, in other words, destroy him who had the power of death, the devil. This can be seen also in I John 3:8: "For this purpose the Son of God was manifested, that He might destroy the works of the devil."

Death Is Separation

In Scripture death always refers to some kind of separation. James wrote, "For as the body without the spirit is dead, so faith without works is dead also" (James 2:26). Physical death occurs when the human spirit and body are separated. So what did Paul mean when he wrote, "And you He made alive, who were dead in trespasses and sins" (Ephesians 2:1)? This is a description of the human condition when we are separated from fellowship with God by our sins. And this is what God referred to when He told Adam, "Of every tree of the garden you may freely eat; but of the tree of the knowledge of good and evil you shall not eat, for in the day that you eat of it you shall surely die" (Genesis 2:16-17). This was not a reference to physical death; Adam lived to be 930 years old.[16] Instead, God's warning was about the spiritual death Adam would experience if he sinned. As a consequence of his spiritual death—his separation from fellowship with God—Adam also experienced physical death, for he was barred from the Garden of Eden and the Tree of Life so he would not live forever in a physical body in a less than ideal state.[17]

In order to obtain redemption for us, it was necessary for Christ to fully embrace human existence and the human experience. This included the experience of death. As Gregory of Nazianzus, a fourth-century Christian theologian said, "The unassumed is the unhealed." His point was if there is anything about essential humanity that was not experienced by Christ, that aspect of human existence was not included in Christ's redemptive work. Here is how Paul put it in Philippians 2:5-11: "Let this mind be in you which was also in Christ Jesus, who, being in the form of God, did not consider it robbery to be equal with God, but made Himself of no reputation, taking the form of a bondservant, and coming in the likeness of men. And being found in appearance as a man, He humbled Himself and became obedient to the point of death, even the death of the cross. Therefore God also has highly exalted Him and given Him the name which is above every name, that at the name of Jesus every knee should bow, of those in heaven, and of those on earth, and of those under the earth, and that every tongue should confess that Jesus Christ is Lord, to the glory of God the Father."

The prophesied enmity between the serpent and Eve's descendant would result in death for both of them, but the Messiah, the Seed of the woman, would rise from the dead. For Satan, there would be no resurrection. His eternal destiny is to be cast into the lake of fire and brimstone, where he will be tormented day and night forever and ever (Revelation 20:10).

Death Is Swallowed Up in Victory

By virtue of Christ's resurrection, "Death is swallowed up in victory" (I Corinthians 15:54). In I Corinthians 15:55 Paul followed these words with a quote from Hosea 13:14: "O Death, where is your sting? O Hades, where is your victory?" Then, Paul continued, "The sting of death is sin, and the strength of sin is the law. But thanks be to God, who gives us the victory through our Lord Jesus Christ" (I Corinthians 15:56-58). Christ's victory over death becomes our victory over death. Because Christ stands in solidarity with us, we are united with Him in His death, burial, and resurrection. Paul explained it this way: "Do you not know that as many of us as were baptized into Christ Jesus were baptized into His death? Therefore we were buried with Him through baptism into death, that just as Christ was raised from the dead by the glory of the Father, even so we also should walk in newness of life. For if we have been united together in the likeness of His death, certainly we also shall be in the likeness of His resurrection, knowing this, that our old man was crucified with Him, that the body of sin might be done away with, that we should no longer be slaves of sin. For he who has died has been freed from sin. Now if we died with Christ, we believe that we shall also live with Him, knowing that Christ, having been raised from the dead, dies no more. Death no longer has dominion over Him. For the death that He died, He died to sin once for all; but the life that He lives, He lives to God. Likewise you also, reckon yourselves to be dead indeed to sin, but alive to God in Christ Jesus our Lord" (Romans 6:3-11).

We have been discussing intertextuality, or the way later Scripture uses earlier Scripture. A fascinating example of this is Paul's use of Hosea 13:14 in I Corinthians 15:55, where Paul quotes Hosea to point out that the resurrection has taken the sting out of death and victory from the grave. In Hosea 13:14, the LORD declares in a very dramatic way that He will destroy death and the grave: "I will ransom them from the power of the grave; I will redeem them from death. O Death, I will be your plagues! O Grave, I will be your destruction!" In the New Testament Jesus said, "I am the Resurrection and the life. He who believes in Me, though he may die, he shall live" (John 11:25).

It is true that the serpent dealt a deathblow to the Messiah's heel. But he could do this only because the Messiah was willing to place His foot on the serpent's head, thus delivering a crushing and deadly wound from which the serpent would never recover. Meanwhile, the Messiah, our Lord and Savior Jesus Christ, would live again. Death could not keep Him! The grave could not hold Him! In the words of Charles Wesley's timeless hymn, "Christ Our

Lord Is Risen Today," "Love's redeeming work is done ...
fought the fight, the battle won ... death in vain forbids
Him rise ... Christ has opened Paradise. Alleluia!"

3

Jacob's Prophecy to Judah

As we seek to grow in the knowledge of our Lord and Savior Jesus Christ through the testimony about Him in the Hebrew Scriptures, we must be alert to quotations from, allusions to, or paraphrases of Old Testament texts found in the New Testament. One such reference is located in Matthew 21. Beginning with the first verse, Matthew wrote these words: "Now when they drew near Jerusalem, and came to Bethphage, at the Mount of Olives, then Jesus sent two disciples, saying to them, 'Go into the village opposite you, and immediately you will find a donkey tied, and a colt with her. Loose them and bring them to Me. And if anyone says anything to you, you shall say, "The Lord has need of them," and immediately he will send them.' All this was done that it might be fulfilled which was spoken by the prophet, saying: 'Tell the daughter of Zion, behold, your King is coming to you, lowly, and sitting on a donkey, a colt, the foal of a donkey.' So the disciples went and did as Jesus commanded them. They brought the donkey and the colt, laid their clothes on them, and set Him on them. And a very great multitude spread their clothes on the road; others cut down branches from the trees and spread them on the road. Then the multitudes who went before and those who followed cried out, saying: 'Hosanna to the Son of David! Blessed is He who comes in the name of the LORD! Hosanna in the highest!' And when He had come into Jerusalem, all the city was moved, saying, 'Who is this?' So the multitudes said, 'This is Jesus, the prophet from Nazareth of Galilee'" (Matthew 21:1-11).

Matthew and Zechariah

When Matthew wrote, "All this was done that it might be fulfilled which was spoken by the prophet," he was quoting from Zechariah 9:9. The prophet wrote, "Rejoice greatly, O daughter of Zion! Shout, O daughter of Jerusalem! Behold, your King is coming to you; He is just and having salvation, lowly and riding on a donkey, a colt, the foal of a donkey." This is an example of intertextuality, where a later writer in Scripture quotes from an earlier writer in an interpretive way. In this case, Matthew declared Jesus to be the King of whom Zechariah wrote. But notice it was first Jesus Himself who claimed to fulfill this prophecy by sending His disciples to find the donkey and colt and telling them what to say if anyone questioned their actions.

Zechariah and Genesis

It is fascinating that the prophecy found in Zechariah is itself drawn from a much earlier prophetic statement made by Jacob in his last words to his twelve sons. After making a series of negative statements about Reuben,

Simeon, and Levi, Jacob said to Judah: "You are he whom your brothers shall praise; your hand shall be on the neck of your enemies; your father's children shall bow down before you. Judah is a lion's whelp; from the prey, my son, you have gone up. He bows down, he lies down as a lion; and as a lion, who shall rouse him? The scepter shall not depart from Judah, nor a lawgiver from between his feet, until Shiloh comes; and to Him shall be the obedience of the people. Binding his foal[18] to the vine, and his donkey's colt to the choice vine, he washed his garments in wine, and his clothes in the blood of grapes. His eyes are darker than wine, and his teeth whiter than milk" (Genesis 49:8-12). Genesis 49:11 and Zechariah 9:9 are the only two places in the Old Testament where the words "foal" and "colt" are found together. The only other place where they are found together in the entire Bible is in Matthew 21:2, 5, 7. This is an excellent example of intertextuality. First, the words are found in Genesis, then they are found and further clarified in Zechariah, and finally they are found again in Matthew, where they are specifically said to be fulfilled in Christ. In retrospect we can see that they had to do with Christ all along, even in Genesis 49. As Jesus told his disciples, everything that is written concerning Him in the law of Moses—a reference to Genesis, Exodus, Leviticus, Numbers, and Deuteronomy—must be fulfilled.[19] Since we know now the Messiah is the ultimate reference in Jacob's dying words to Judah, let's look at that prophecy more carefully.

Judah's Blessing

First, notice that even though Judah was not Jacob's firstborn son—he was born fourth, with Leah as his mother—he is given preeminence over all the other eleven sons. Jacob said, "Judah, you are he whom your brothers shall praise; your hand shall be on the neck of your enemies; your father's children shall bow down before you" (Genesis 49:8). Here is the way it was put by the chronicler: "Now the sons of Reuben the firstborn of Israel—he was indeed the firstborn, but because he defiled his father's bed, his birthright was given to the sons of Joseph, the son of Israel, so that the genealogy is not listed according to birthright; yet Judah prevailed over his brothers, and from him came a ruler, although the birthright was Joseph's" (I Chronicles 5:1-2). Asaph explained it this way: "Moreover He rejected the tent of Joseph, and did not choose the tribe of Ephraim, but chose the tribe of Judah, Mount Zion which He loved" (Psalm 78:67-68). So Judah, whose name means "praised," would indeed be praised by his brothers. As a victorious warrior, he would gain the upper hand over his enemies. In acknowledgement of his victory, his brothers would bow down before him. This reminds us of Joseph's dream, which was fulfilled in Egypt, but ultimately this would come true for Judah, when even the descendants of Joseph would bow before a descendant of Judah. It does not take a great deal of imagination to see in Jacob's words the anticipation of David's ascent to the throne of Israel. David was, of course, of the tribe of Judah.

The Lion of the Tribe of Judah

In Genesis 49:9, the imagery moves from portraying Judah as a victorious warrior to presenting him as a lion: "Judah is a lion's whelp; from the prey, my son, you have gone up. He bows down, he lies down as a lion; and as a lion, who shall rouse him?" Like a lion that has finished eating his prey, he lies down. Because he is powerful and dangerous to his enemies, no one dares to rouse him. In a remarkable example of intertextuality, we find these same words on the lips of Balaam. Balak had hired Balaam to curse Israel, but Balaam could speak only the words that God put in his mouth. These words included the following prophecy of the coming Messiah: "God brings him out of Egypt; he has strength like a wild ox; he shall consume the nations, his enemies; he shall break their bones and pierce them with his arrows. He bows down, he lies down as a lion; and as a lion, who shall rouse him?" (Numbers 24:8-9). John was influenced by these prophecies when he described the scene in heaven's throne room: "And I saw in the right hand of Him who sat on the throne a scroll written inside and on the back, sealed with seven seals. Then I saw a strong angel proclaiming with a loud voice, 'Who is worthy to open the scroll and to loose its seals?' And no one in heaven or on the earth or under the earth was able to open the scroll, or to look at it. So I wept much, because no one was found worthy to open and read the scroll, or to look at it. But one of the elders said to me, 'Do not weep. Behold, the Lion of the tribe of Judah, the Root of David, has prevailed to open the scroll and to loose its seven seals'" (Revelation 5:1-5). In the first book of the Bible, Genesis, Judah's victorious descendant is described as a lion; in the last book of the Bible, Revelation, Jesus is identified as the Lion of the tribe of Judah. This is an excellent example of intertextuality, and it shows how the use of early Scripture in later biblical books serves to explain or interpret the previous texts.

Judah's Scepter

In Genesis 49:10, Jacob's description of Judah moves from a lion to a king. Jacob said, "The scepter shall not depart from Judah, nor a lawgiver from between his feet, until Shiloh comes; and to Him shall be the obedience of the people." The scepter is a symbol of kingly rule. Israel's first king would not be from the tribe of Judah. Saul was from the tribe of Benjamin. But Saul was placed on Israel's throne because the people of Israel had rejected God's rule.[20] God's intention was that Israel's first king would be from the tribe of Judah. In accepting a king from the tribe of Judah, Israel would not be rejecting God. Nevertheless, in spite of the premature choice of Saul, Jacob's prophetic words still retained their integrity, for he did not say there would never be a king over Israel from another tribe; he said the scepter would not *depart* from Judah. In other words, once the scepter was in the hand of a king from the tribe of Judah, there would never be a king from another tribe. Although, in the later history of Israel, there were various political maneuverings attempting to place rulers on the throne who were not from the tribe of Judah, all such were pretenders who did not rule with divine authority. When the integrity and godliness of the rulers from the tribe of Judah degenerated to the point that they were removed from the throne, the throne, rather than being handed to another tribe, was left vacant, awaiting the arrival of the final and ultimate King who would be of the tribe of Judah. This came about because of God's rejection of Coniah, also known as Jeconiah. Coniah was so wicked that the prophet Jeremiah wrote, "Is this man Coniah a despised, broken idol—a vessel in which is no pleasure? Why are they cast out, he and his descendants, and cast into a land which they do not know? O earth, earth, earth, hear the word of the LORD! Thus says the LORD: 'Write this man down as childless, a man who shall not prosper in his days; for none of his descendants shall prosper, sitting on the throne of David, and ruling anymore in Judah'" (Jeremiah 22:28-30). Concerning this vacating of the throne, the prophet Hosea wrote, "For the children of Israel shall abide many days without king or prince, without sacrifice or sacred pillar, without ephod or teraphim. Afterward the children of Israel shall return and seek the LORD their God and David their king. They shall fear the LORD and His goodness in the latter days" (Hosea 3:4-5). David had been dead for 207 years when Hosea wrote this prophecy. So Hosea's prophecy anticipated the coming of the ultimate and final Davidic King, the Messiah, Jesus Christ. In the meantime, no one else would sit on David's throne. As Jacob had said many years before, "The scepter shall not depart from Judah, nor a lawgiver from between his feet, until Shiloh comes; and to Him shall be the obedience of the people" (Genesis 49:10).

Until Shiloh Comes

The word "Shiloh" is simply a transliteration, not a translation, from the Hebrew. The meaning of the word is "one to whom it belongs." This ultimate one to whom the scepter belongs, and whom the people shall obey, is none other than the Messiah, Jesus Christ. It is fascinating to compare the genealogies of Jesus as recorded in Matthew and Luke. From Abraham to David, the genealogies are identical.[21] But when we get to David's descendant, the genealogies diverge. According to Matthew, David's

descendant is Solomon (Matthew 1:6). According to
Luke, David's descendant is Nathan (Luke 3:31). What's
going on here? The answer is that Matthew records the
genealogy of Jesus Christ through Joseph. Joseph was a
descendant of David through Solomon and thus through
Jeconiah (Matthew 1:11). If Joseph had been the biological father of Jesus, this would have disqualified Jesus
from sitting on the throne of David, for Jeremiah had
said, "Write this man down as childless, a man who shall
not prosper in his days; for none of his descendants shall
prosper, sitting on the throne of David, and ruling anymore in Judah." On the other hand, Luke records the
genealogy of Jesus through Mary, who was the biological
mother of Jesus. Mary was also a descendant of David, but
not through Solomon and thus not through Jeconiah. She
descended from David through another of David's sons,
Nathan. Thus, Jesus' descent from the tribe of Judah and
from David was preserved through Mary, while avoiding
the problem created by Jeconiah. The angel Gabriel said
to Mary, "Do not be afraid, Mary, for you have found favor
with God. And behold, you will conceive in your womb
and bring forth a Son, and shall call His name JESUS. He
will be great, and will be called the Son of the Highest;
and the Lord God will give Him the throne of His father
David. And He will reign over the house of Jacob forever,
and of His kingdom there will be no end" (Luke 1:30-33).
Jacob had said of Judah that his father's children would
bow down before him. This is fulfilled by Jesus in that He
will reign over the house of Jacob forever. But Jacob had
also said the obedience of the people would be to Judah's
descendant, the one to whom the throne belonged. The
word translated "people" (*'ammim*) refers not just to

Israel, the descendants of Jacob, but to the nations of the world. In the prophetic declaration of Psalm 2:7-8, the Messiah said, "I will declare the decree: The LORD has said to me, 'You are My Son, today I have begotten You. Ask of Me, and I will give you the nations for Your inheritance, and the ends of the earth for your possession." In Revelation 5 the four living creatures and the twenty-four elders fall down before the Lamb, who is also identified as the Lion of the tribe of Judah and the Root of David, and they sing this new song: "You are worthy to take the scroll, and to open its seals; for You were slain, and have redeemed us to God by Your blood out of every tribe and tongue and people and nation" (Revelation 5:9).

The Donkey and the Colt

Now we come to Jacob's description of Judah's descendant as one who binds his donkey to the vine. Jacob said, "Binding his donkey to the vine, and his donkey's colt to the choice vine, he washed his garments in wine, and his clothes in the blood of grapes. His eyes are darker than wine, and his teeth whiter than milk." This is the imagery that connects verbally with Zechariah 9:9 and Matthew 21:2, 5, 7. It is the imagery of blessing and prosperity. To say He will bind His donkey to the vine and his donkey's colt to the choice vine indicates the best of vines will be so common that one would not mind tethering one's donkey to them, even though the donkey may eat some of the grapes while tethered there. To say He washes His garments in wine and his clothes in the blood of grapes indicates that wine will be as plentiful as wash water.[22] The description of this King as having eyes darker than wine and teeth whiter than milk suggests He is a strong, powerful King.

57

Isaiah and Revelation

We have already seen how the words of Jacob to his son Judah are appropriated by Zechariah, by Jesus Himself, and by Matthew in a messianic way. But that is not all: we also see echoes of Jacob's words in Isaiah and Revelation. Isaiah 63 opens with a question: "Who is this who comes from Edom, with dyed garments from Bozrah, this One who is glorious in His apparel, traveling in the greatness of His strength?" Then the answer comes, "I who speak in righteousness, mighty to save." Then another question: "Why is Your apparel red, and Your garments like one who treads in the winepress?" The answer is, "I have trodden the winepress alone, and from the peoples no one was with Me. For I have trodden them in My anger, and trampled them in My fury; their blood is sprinkled upon My garments, and I have stained all my robes. For the day of vengeance is in My heart, and the year of My redeemed has come. I looked, but there was no one to help, and I wondered that there was no one to uphold; therefore My own arm brought salvation for Me; and My own fury, it sustained me" (Isaiah 63:1-5). Jacob's references to the blood of grapes and to the washing of garments in wine become for Isaiah a picture of the red color of Messiah's garments, a color that suggested he had been treading in the winepress. But the winepress is only a figure of speech; the Messiah has trodden a winepress of judgment against those who rejected Him, resulting in His garments being sprinkled with their blood.

Next, Jacob's words, as they are appropriated by Isaiah, are used by John in his description of the Second Coming. John wrote, "Now I saw heaven opened, and behold, a white horse. And He who sat on him was called Faithful and True, and in righteousness He judges and makes war. His eyes were like a flame of fire, and on His head were many crowns. He had a name written that no one knew except Himself. He was clothed with a robe dipped in blood, and His name is called The Word of God. And the armies in heaven, clothed in fine linen, white and clean, followed Him on white horses. Now out of His mouth goes a sharp sword, that with it He should strike the nations. And He Himself will rule them with a rod of iron. He Himself treads the winepress of the fierceness and wrath of Almighty God. And He has on His robe and on His thigh a name written: KING OF KINGS AND LORD OF LORDS" (Revelation 19:11-16.).

Notice the connections between this grand description of the Messiah's return, Jacob's original prophetic statement to Judah, and Isaiah's appropriation of Jacob's prophecy:

Reading Between the Lines

Jacob	Isaiah	John
He washes His garments in wine, the blood of grapes.	The redness of the Messiah's garments is not due to wine, but to His victory over His enemies as His garments were sprinkled with their blood.	Jesus is clothed with a robe dipped in blood.
His eyes are darker than wine.		His eyes are like a flame of fire.
His teeth are whiter than milk, indicating strength and power.		A sharp sword goes out of His mouth with which He strikes the nations.
He binds His donkey to the vine and His donkey's colt to the choice vine.		He rides on a white horse.
The scepter never departs from Him.		He has on His head many crowns.
His hand is on the neck of His enemies, and to Him shall be the obedience of the nations.		He judges and makes war in righteousness, striking the nations and ruling them with a rod of iron.
	The appearance of the Messiah's clothing as of one who treads out the winepress represents the Messiah as He treads the winepress of God's judgment.	Jesus treads the winepress of the fierceness and wrath of Almighty God.

When Jesus rode into Jerusalem on the back of a donkey, it was in fulfillment of Zechariah 9:9. But Zechariah was not the only prophet to be influenced by Jacob's words as he pronounced a blessing over Judah. Isaiah was also influenced by them, with a longer view than Zechariah. The ultimate and final fulfillment of Jacob's prophetic blessing will come when our Lord Jesus Christ makes His second appearance, riding from heaven on a white horse, clothed with the bloody robe of a victorious conqueror, coming in final and complete victory over all who have opposed Him, the KING OF KINGS AND THE LORD OF LORDS.

Just before His departure from this earth, Jesus told His disciples that everything written concerning Him in the law of Moses must be fulfilled. We can be sure Jacob's last words of blessing over his son Judah will be fulfilled when Judah's greatest Son, our Lord and Savior, Jesus Christ, appears in glory. Judah's brothers will praise Him; His hand will be on the neck of His enemies; and Jacob's children will bow down before Him, just as Jacob anticipated on that day so long ago.

4

The Passover

After the first nine of the ten plagues, Pharaoh still refused to release the people of Israel. So the LORD said to Moses, "I will bring one more plague on Pharaoh and on Egypt. Afterward he will let you go from here. When he lets you go, he will surely drive you out of here altogether" (Exodus 11:1). This plague would be the most severe of them all. The LORD said, "About midnight I will go out into the midst of Egypt; and all the firstborn in the land of Egypt shall die, from the firstborn of Pharaoh who sits on his throne, even to the firstborn of the female servant who is behind the handmill, and all the firstborn of the animals" (Exodus 11:4-5). There was only one way that even the Israelites could escape this terrible plague. Each household must select a male lamb in its first year of life, making sure the lamb had no blemish. On the fourteenth day of the month, at twilight, the lamb was to be killed and some of its blood applied to the two doorposts and the lintel of the house where the lamb would be eaten.[23]

The LORD said, "I will pass through the land of Egypt on that night, and will strike all the firstborn in the land of Egypt, both man and beast; and against all the gods of Egypt I will execute judgment: I am the LORD. Now the blood shall be a sign for you on the houses where you are. And when I see the blood, I will pass over you; and the plague shall not be on you to destroy you when I strike the land of Egypt" (Exodus 12:12-13).

Thus was born the celebration known as the Passover, which was to be commemorated each year. Moses said, "For the LORD will pass through to strike the Egyptians; and when He sees the blood on the lintel and on the two doorposts, the LORD will pass over the door and not allow the destroyer to come into your houses to strike you. And you shall observe this thing as an ordinance for you and your sons forever. It will come to pass when you come to the land which the LORD will give you, just as He promised, that you shall keep this service. And it shall be, when your children say to you, 'What do you mean by this service?' that you shall say, 'It is the Passover sacrifice of the LORD, who passed over the houses of the children of Israel in Egypt when He struck the Egyptians and delivered our households'" (Exodus 12:23-27).

The annual observance of the Passover would be in conjunction with the Feast of Unleavened Bread. On the same day that the lamb had been killed at the first Passover, the Feast of Unleavened Bread began.[24] For seven days, the Israelites were to eat nothing with leaven, or yeast.

Jesus and the Passover

It was at the annual observance of the Passover that Jesus said to His disciples, "Assuredly, I say to you, one of you will betray Me" (Matthew 26:21). The disciples were very sorry and each asked, "Lord, is it I?" (Matthew 26:22). Jesus answered, "He who dipped his hand with Me in the dish will betray Me" (Matthew 26:23). Judas asked, "Rabbi, is it I?" Jesus replied, "You have said it" (Matthew 26:25).

As Jesus and His disciples were eating the Passover meal, Jesus took bread, blessed and broke it, and gave it to the disciples with these words, "Take, eat; this is My body" (Matthew 26:26). Then He took the cup, gave thanks, and gave it to the disciples, saying, "Drink from it, all of you. For this is My blood of the new covenant, which is shed for many for the remission of sins" (Matthew 26:27-28). Why did Jesus do these things and make this statement on the night of the Passover?

Later, after His betrayal, crucifixion, burial, and resurrection, Jesus appeared to His disciples and said, "These are the words which I spoke to you while I was still with you, that all things must be fulfilled which were written in the Law of Moses and the Prophets and the Psalms concerning Me" (Luke 24:44). Could it be that the Passover lamb was in some way a prophetic symbol of the coming Messiah?

The Lamb of God

When John the Baptist began his ministry, representatives from the Pharisees were sent to him, asking, "Why ... do you baptize if you are not the Christ, nor Elijah, nor the Prophet?" (John 1:25). John answered, "I baptize with water, but there stands One among you whom you do not know. It is He who, coming after me, is preferred before me, whose sandal straps I am not worthy to loose" (John 1:26-27).

The next day John saw Jesus coming toward him, and said, "Behold! The Lamb of God who takes away the sin of the world! This is He of whom I said, 'After me comes a Man who is preferred before me, for He was before me.' I did not know Him; but that He should be revealed to Israel, therefore I came baptizing with water" (John 1:29-31). Further, John said, "I saw the Spirit descending from heaven like a dove, and He remained upon Him. I did not know Him, but He who sent me to baptize with water said to me, 'Upon whom you see the Spirit descending, and remaining on Him, this is He who baptizes with the Holy Spirit.' And I have seen and testified that this is the Son of God" (John 1:32-34). The next day, John said to two of his disciples as Jesus walked by, "Behold the Lamb of God!" (John 1:35-36).

So, early in his ministry, John the Baptist twice identified Jesus as the Lamb of God. Further, it is as the Lamb of God that Jesus takes away the sin of the world.

Christ, Our Passover

Another clue that the Passover lamb represented Jesus in some way is found in Paul's first letter to the church in Corinth. After issuing a stern warning about their toleration of unusual sexual immorality, Paul wrote, "Your glorying is not good. Do you not know that a little leaven leavens the whole lump? Therefore purge out the old leaven, that you may be a new lump, since you truly are unleavened. For indeed Christ, our Passover, was sacrificed for us. Therefore let us keep the feast, not with old leaven, nor with the leaven of malice and wickedness, but with the unleavened bread of sincerity and truth" (I Corinthians 5:6-8). Clearly, Paul was drawing on the imagery of the original Passover, when a spotless lamb was slain and its blood was applied to the doorposts and lintel of the homes of the Israelites so they could be spared the terror of the tenth plague. He was also using imagery associated with the Feast of Unleavened Bread, which was to be observed annually beginning with the first anniversary of the first Passover.

The Lamb as It Had Been Slain

In a breathtaking vision of the heavenly throne room, John "saw in the right hand of Him who sat on the throne a scroll written inside and on the back, sealed with seven seals" (Revelation 5:1). Then John "saw a strong angel proclaiming with a loud voice, 'Who is worthy to open the scroll and to loose its seals?' And no one in heaven or on the earth or under the earth was able to open the scroll or to look at it" (Revelation 5:2-3). Then he wept profusely "because no one was found worthy to open and read the scroll, or to look at it" (Revelation 5:4). But then one of the elders said to John, "Do not weep. Behold, the Lion of the tribe of Judah, the Root of David, has prevailed to open the scroll and to loose its seven seals" (Revelation 5:5). But when John looked, what he saw in the midst of the throne and of the four living creatures, and in the midst of the elders, did not look like a lion. He saw "a Lamb as though it had been slain, having seven horns and seven eyes" (Revelation 5:6).

The Book of Revelation records a visionary experience that John had while "in the Spirit on the Lord's Day" (Revelation 1:10). Visions are symbolic; that which is seen in biblical visions represents a greater reality not visible to human eyes. In this case, the Lamb John saw looked as though it had been slain. But it was not dead; the Lamb came and took the scroll from the hand of Him who sat on the throne. John tells us that the seven horns and seven eyes of the Lamb represent the seven Spirits of God sent out into all the earth (Revelation 5:6). This may be a reference to Isaiah 11:2, where the Spirit of the Lord that rests upon the Messiah may be described as a seven-branched candelabra. The Spirit of the LORD is the central shaft, from which extends the Spirit of wisdom, the Spirit of understanding, the Spirit of counsel, the Spirit of might, the Spirit of knowledge, and the Spirit of the fear of the Lord.

In John's vision, after the Lamb took the scroll, the four living creatures and the twenty-four elders who were gathered around the throne "fell down before the Lamb, each having a harp, and golden bowls full of incense, which are the prayers of the saints" (Revelation 5:8). And they sang this new song to the Lamb: "You are worthy to take the scroll, and to open its seals; for You were slain, and have redeemed us to God by Your blood out of every tribe and tongue and people and nation, and have made us kings and priests to our God; and we shall reign on the earth" (Revelation 5:9-10). John looked and heard the voice of many angels around the throne, including the living creatures and the elders. The angels numbered ten thousand times ten thousand, and thousands of thousands.[25] With a loud voice, these angels said, "Worthy is the Lamb who was slain to receive power and riches and wisdom and strength and honor and glory and blessing!" (Revelation 5:12).

Then John heard every creature which is in heaven and on the earth and under the earth and in the sea, saying, "Blessing and honor and glory and power be to Him who sits on the throne and to the Lamb, forever and ever!" (Revelation 5:13). Then the four living creatures said, "Amen!" And the twenty-four elders fell down and worshiped Him who lives forever and ever (Revelation 5:14). Following this, the Lamb began to open the seals (Revelation 6:1).

When we read the Book of Revelation, it is important that we remember it reports a visionary experience. Otherwise we may think that heaven is populated with strange, talking creatures, and we may wonder how One who is described as a Lion could also be described as a Lamb, and especially as a slain Lamb with seven horns and seven eyes. We may also think the One who sits on the throne and the Lamb are two distinct beings, since the Lamb comes to take the scroll from the right hand of the One sitting on the throne. But as we keep reading, many of these questions are resolved as the vision unfolds. For example, we have already learned that the seven horns and seven eyes do not describe literal horns and eyes, but the seven Spirits of God.

Later in his vision, John saw "a beast rising up out of the sea, having seven heads and ten horns, and on his horns ten crowns, and on his heads a blasphemous name" (Revelation 13:1). This beast "was like a leopard, his feet were like the feet of a bear, and his mouth was like the mouth of a lion" (Revelation 13:2). Everyone dwelling on earth worships this beast, "whose names have not been written in the Book of Life of the Lamb slain from the foundation of the world" (Revelation 13:8). Ultimately, after the return of the Messiah, the beast is captured and cast alive into the lake of fire burning with brimstone.[26]

Who is this Lamb that John saw in his vision? You have probably already guessed that the Lamb represents our Lord and Savior, Jesus Christ. Just as John the Baptist identified Jesus as the Lamb of God who takes away the sin of the world, and just as Paul identified Him as our Passover Lamb, so John described Him as a slain Lamb, a reference to His death on the cross. But according to John, the Lamb was slain "from the foundation of the world" (Revelation 13:8). How could this be? Although Jesus was not crucified until a specific point in time, the cross was God's plan of redemption from the very beginning of creation. Since He knew even before He created them that people would fall into sin, God made provision for people to be restored to Him—and He made this provision even before He created Adam and Eve. Some people wonder why God created human beings if He knew in advance that they would sin. But the problem posed by that question is resolved when we realize that God arranged for the redemption of human beings even before they came into existence. Jesus Christ was the Lamb slain from the foundation of the world. Even those who lived and died before Christ came could enjoy the benefits of redemption provided by the Cross. In an apparent allusion to the Passover lamb, Paul wrote that believers are "justified freely by His grace through the redemption that is in Christ Jesus, whom God set forth as a propitiation by His blood, through faith, to demonstrate His righteousness, because in His forbearance God had passed over the sins that were previously committed" (Romans 3:24-25). The words "passed over" connect conceptually with the Passover lamb. The people who had obeyed the commandment to kill a spotless lamb and to put the lamb's blood on their doorposts and on the lintel of their homes were spared the consequences of the tenth plague as the death angel "passed over" their homes. Likewise, those people of faith who lived before Christ came benefited in advance from the shedding of Christ's blood as God "passed over the sins that were previously committed." Those of us who live after Christ came are also justified by His blood, and we have the promise that "we shall be saved from wrath through Him" (Romans 5:9).

Philip Interprets Isaiah

When Philip encountered the treasurer of Ethiopia on the road leading from Jerusalem to Gaza, the Ethiopian was reading from the prophet Isaiah. The Holy Spirit spoke to Philip, saying, "Go near and overtake this chariot" (Acts 8:29). Running to the man, Philip heard him reading aloud from Isaiah, and asked, "Do you understand what you are reading?" (Acts 8:30). The government official responded, "How can I, unless someone guides me?" (Acts 8:31). Then he asked Philip to join him in his chariot. The Ethiopian was reading these words from Isaiah 53:7-8: "He was led as a sheep to the slaughter; and as a lamb before its shearer is silent, so He opened not His mouth. In His humiliation His justice was taken away, and who will declare His generation? For His life is taken from the earth" (Acts 8:32-33). He said to Philip, "I ask you, of whom does the prophet say this, of himself or of some other man?" (Acts 8:34). Beginning with Isaiah's prophecy about a lamb, Philip preached Jesus to the Ethiopian. He explained Isaiah's prophecy so clearly that when the chariot approached a body of water, the Ethiopian treasurer said, "See, here is water, what hinders me from being baptized?" (Acts 8:36). Philip answered, "If you believe with all your heart, you may." And he answered and said, "I believe that Jesus Christ is the Son of God" (Acts 8:37). The two men got out of the chariot and went down into the water, where Philip baptized the man from Ethiopia.[27]

It is important for us to note that the Ethiopian was reading from Isaiah 53, one of the most extensive and clear prophecies about the coming Messiah and His redemptive work. In His work of bearing our transgressions, He is described as a lamb and a sheep. Philip was not the only one who understood this. Peter wrote that we arc "not redeemed with corruptible things, like silver or gold ... but with the precious blood of Christ, as of a lamb without blemish and without spot" (I Peter 1:18-19). In agreement with John's statement that the Lamb was slain from the foundation of the world, Peter continued, "He indeed was foreordained before the foundation of the world, but was manifest in these last times for you who through Him believe in God, who raised Him from the dead and gave Him glory, so that your faith and hope are in God" (I Peter 1:20-21).

The Lamb and the One on the Throne

In John's vision the Lamb took the scroll from the hand of the One who was sitting on the throne. Does this mean that the Lamb and the One sitting on the throne are distinct beings? Obviously the One on the throne is God, but then who is the Lamb?

After his vision of the New Jerusalem, John wrote, "But I saw no temple in it, for the Lord God Almighty and the Lamb are its temple" (Revelation 21:22). Does this indicate that the Lord God Almighty is someone other than the Lamb or that the Lamb is not the Lord God Almighty? A glance at the inspired Greek text helps us with this question. The Greek word translated "are" in the phrase "are its temple" is the third person singular form of the Greek "to be" verb. The verb is *eimi*, and the third person singular form, *estin*, means "is." In the Greek language, singular subjects take singular verbs, and plural subjects take plural verbs. Why, then, is the phrase "the Lord God Almighty and the Lamb" accompanied by the singular verb in the Greek text? Why do the translators render it as if the verb were plural? First, the singular verb indicates the phrase "the Lord God Almighty and the Lamb" form one subject; they are one and the same. Thus, a singular verb is required. But it would sound quite awkward in English translation to render the words "the Lord God Almighty and the Lamb is its temple," so many translations render the singular verb as if it were plural. Some translations avoid this problem, however, with translations like "for its temple is the Lord God Almighty and the Lamb" (RSV).

Because of what follows in John's Revelation, we do know the Lamb is none other than the Lord God Almighty. In the final chapter of the book, John wrote, "And he showed me a pure river of water of life, clear as crystal, proceeding from the throne of God and of the Lamb. ...And there shall be no more curse, but the throne of God and of the Lamb shall be in it, and His servants shall serve Him. They shall see His face, and His name shall be on their foreheads" (Revelation 22:1, 3-4). Notice how the phrase "God and the Lamb" is referred to by the singular pronoun. The pronoun "His" is used in reference to the one face and the one name of God and of the Lamb. The one throne is the throne of God and of the Lamb; His servants, not their servants, serve Him, not them. In other words, as we continue to read the Book of Revelation, the slain yet living Lamb of Revelation 5, the Lamb with seven horns and seven eyes, turns out to be none other than the Lord God Almighty Himself. Although John has seen the results of the Lamb's redemptive role portrayed in dramatic symbolism, we discover in the latter pages of John's vision that the Lamb of God is none other than God Himself, occupying the throne of heaven.

This is wonderfully described by Paul, who said, in his parting words to the elders of the church in Ephesus, "Take heed to yourselves and to all the flock, among which the Holy Spirit has made you overseers, to shepherd the church of God, which He purchased with His own blood" (Acts 20:28). The One who purchased the church with His own blood was God. But in the miracle of the Incarnation, God was manifest in human existence, making it possible for Him to shed His own blood and thus to pass over our sins, as was anticipated by the blood of the Passover lamb, which spared the ancient Israelites from the painful consequence of the tenth plague.

5

Balaam's Prophecy

It may be that one of the most unexpected prophecies about the coming Messiah was given by a mercenary prophet. When Balak, the king of the Moabites, saw how the Israelites had defeated the Amorites in battle, he contacted Balaam with this message: "Look, a people has come from Egypt. See, they cover the face of the earth, and are settling next to me! Therefore please come at once, curse this people for me, for they are too mighty for me. Perhaps I shall be able to defeat them and drive them out of the land, for I know that he whom you bless is blessed, and he whom you curse is cursed" (Numbers 22:5-6). Balak's representatives relayed his message to Balaam, offering him a fee for his services. Balaam said, "Lodge here tonight, and I will bring back word to you, as the LORD speaks to me" (Numbers 22:8).

While Balak's representatives stayed with Balaam, God came to Balaam and asked, "Who are these men with you?" (Numbers 22:9). Balaam answered, "Balak the son of Zippor, king of Moab, has sent to me, saying, 'Look, a people has come out of Egypt, and they cover the face of the earth. Come now, curse them for me; perhaps I shall be able to overpower them and drive them out'" (Numbers 22:10-11). God told Balaam, "You shall not go with them; you shall not curse the people, for they are blessed" (Numbers 22:12). The next morning Balaam told Balak's representatives, "Go back to your land, for the LORD has refused to give me permission to go with you" (Numbers 23:13). But when Balak learned of Balaam's decision, he refused to give up. Instead, he sent more princes who were more honorable than his previous representatives, who appealed to Balaam by saying, "Thus says Balak the son of Zippor: 'Please let nothing hinder you from coming to me; for I will certainly honor you greatly, and I will do whatever you say to me. Therefore please come, curse this people for me'" (Numbers 22:16-17). Balaam answered, "Though Balak were to give me his house full of silver and gold, I could not go beyond the word of the LORD my God, to do less or more. Now therefore, please, you also stay here tonight, that I may know what more the LORD will say to me" (Numbers 22:18-19). That night, God said to Balaam, "If the men come to call you, rise and go with them; but only the word which I speak to you—that you shall do" (Numbers 22:20). In the morning, Balaam saddled his donkey and went with the princes of Moab.

The Talking Donkey

The well-known story of the talking donkey comes at this point. As Balaam rode toward Moab, the angel of the LORD stood in the way with a drawn sword. When Balaam's donkey saw the angel, the donkey left the road and went out into the field to avoid the angel. Balaam, who did not see the angel, struck his donkey in an attempt to get it back on the road. But where the road narrowed with walls on both sides, the donkey saw the angel of the LORD again. When the donkey crushed Balaam's foot in a second attempt to avoid the angel by pressing up against the wall, Balaam struck her again. Finally, when the angel stood in an even narrower place in the road where it was impossible to turn to the right or to the left, the donkey lay down under Balaam. In anger, Balaam struck the donkey once more. Then, miraculously, the LORD enabled the donkey to talk. She said to Balaam, "What have I done to you, that you have struck me these three times?" (Numbers 22:28). Balaam, who was apparently so angry that he paid no attention to the oddity of a talking donkey, replied, "Because you have abused me. I wish there were a sword in my hand, for now I would kill you!" (Numbers 22:29). The donkey answered, "Am I not your donkey on which you have ridden, ever since I became yours, to this day? Was I ever disposed to do this to you?" (Numbers 22:30). "No," Balaam said.

After this amazing conversation between Balaam and his donkey, the LORD opened Balaam's eyes, enabling him to see the angel of the Lord with his drawn sword. Balaam fell flat on his face. Then the angel spoke: "Why have you struck your donkey these three times? Behold, I have come out to stand against you, because your way is perverse before Me. The donkey saw me and turned aside from Me these three times. If she had not turned aside from Me, surely I would also have killed you by now, and let her live" (Numbers 22:32-33). Balaam confessed, "I have sinned, for I did not know You stood in the way against me. Now therefore, if it displeases You, I will turn back." Then the angel of the LORD said to Balaam, "Go with the men, but only the word that I speak to you, that you shall speak" (Numbers 22:34-35).

When Balaam arrived in Moab, he said to Balak, "Look, I have come to you! Now, have I any power at all to say anything? The word that God puts in my mouth, that I must speak" (Numbers 22:38). The next day, after offering sacrifices to Baal, Balak took Balaam up to a high place where he could see the extent of the Israelites.

An Unwelcome Message

After offering sacrifices to the LORD, Balaam told Balak to remain behind while he went to see if the LORD would meet him. Balaam said, "Perhaps the LORD will come to meet me, and whatever He shows me I will tell you" (Numbers 23:3). The LORD did give Balaam a message for Balak, but it was not what Balak wanted to hear. Here is what Balaam said: "Balak the king of Moab has brought me from Aram, from the mountains of the east. 'Come, curse Jacob for me, and come, denounce Israel!' How shall I curse whom God has not cursed? And how shall I denounce whom the LORD has not denounced? For from the top of the rocks I see him, and from the hills I behold him; there! A people dwelling alone, not reckoning itself among the nations. Who can count the dust of Jacob, or number one-fourth of Israel? Let me die the death of the righteous, and let my end be like his!" (Numbers 23:7-10).

Balak was furious with Balaam. "What have you done to me?" he asked. "I took you to curse my enemies, and look, you have blessed them bountifully!" (Numbers 23:11). Balaam answered, "Must I not take heed to speak what the LORD has put in my mouth?" (Numbers 23:12).

Then Balak thought if he took Balaam to another place where he could see only a part of the Israelites, perhaps Balaam could curse them. But again, Balaam had bad news for Balak: "Rise up, Balak, and hear! Listen to me, son of Zippor! God is not a man, that He should lie, nor a son of man, that He should repent. Has He said, and will He not do? Or has He spoken, and will He not make it good? Behold, I have received a command to bless; He has blessed, and I cannot reverse it. He has not observed iniquity in Jacob, nor has He seen wickedness in Israel. The LORD his God is with him, and the shout of a King is among them. God brings them out of Egypt; he has strength like a wild ox. For there is no sorcery against Jacob, nor any divination against Israel. It now must be said of Jacob and of Israel, 'Oh, what God has done!' Look, a people rises like a lioness, and lifts itself up like a lion; it shall not lie down until it devours the prey, and drinks the blood of the slain" (Numbers 23:18-24).

The Shout of a King

Balaam said of Israel, "The shout of a King is among them" (Numbers 23:21). Israel had no king at this point; this was a prophetic statement.

After hearing Balaam's second oracle, Balak said, "Neither curse them at all, nor bless them at all!" (Numbers 23:25). Balaam responded, "Did I not tell you, saying, 'All that the LORD speaks, that I must do'?" (Numbers 23:26).

Once again, Balak thought it might work for Balaam to curse Israel if he took Balaam to another location. But when Balaam saw Israel's encampment, the Spirit of God came upon him, and he said: "The utterance of Balaam the son of Beor, the utterance of the man whose eyes are opened, the utterance of him who hears the words of God, who sees the vision of the Almighty, who falls down, with eyes wide open: 'How lovely are your tents, O Jacob! Your dwellings, O Israel! Like valleys that stretch out, like gardens by the riverside, like aloes planted by the LORD, like cedars beside the waters. He shall pour water from his buckets, and his seed shall be in many waters. His king shall be higher than Agag, and his kingdom shall be exalted. God brings him out of Egypt; he has strength like a wild ox; he shall consume the nations, his enemies; He shall break their bones and pierce them through with his arrows. He bows down, he lies down as a lion; and as a lion, who shall rouse him?' Blessed is he who blesses you, and cursed is he who curses you" (Numbers 24:3-9).

God Brings Him Out of Egypt

This oracle of Balaam includes some remarkable prophetic statements about the Messiah. First, there is another reference to Israel's king, although Israel as yet had no king. Second, Balaam said, "God brings him out of Egypt" (Numbers 24:8). We may think at first that this is a reference only to the fact that the Israelites had come out of Egypt. In his second prophecy, Balaam had said, "God brings them out of Egypt" (Numbers 23:22). But now, the prophecy is more specific: "God brings him out of Egypt." We may also think the prophet Hosea referred only to the nation of Israel when he wrote, "When Israel was a child, I loved him, and out of Egypt I called my son" (Hosea 11:1). But for Matthew this was not just a reference to Israel's deliverance from Egypt. When an angel told Joseph to take Mary and Jesus to Egypt to avoid the wrath of Herod, it was, according to Matthew, "that it might be fulfilled which was spoken by the Lord through the prophet, saying, 'Out of Egypt I called My Son'" (Matthew 2:15). By the inspiration of the Holy Spirit, Matthew understood Hosea's prophecy to be about the return of Jesus from Egypt to Israel. Apparently Balaam was interpreting Israel's exodus from Egypt as prophetic of a greater future reality. This seems quite evident in the following words of his third oracle: "He has strength like a wild ox; He shall consume the nations, his enemies; He shall break their bones and pierce them with his arrows" (Numbers 24:8). This is remarkably similar to the messianic prophecy of Psalm 2 where the Messiah said, "I will declare the decree: the LORD has said to Me, 'You are my Son, today I have begotten You. Ask of Me, and I will give you the nations for Your inheritance, and the ends of the earth for your possession. You shall break them with a rod of iron; You shall dash them to pieces like a potter's vessel'" (Psalm 2:7-9).

The Lion of the Tribe of Judah

There can be no question that Balaam's next statement is a messianic prophecy. He said, "He bows down, he lies down as a lion; and as a lion, who shall rouse him?" (Numbers 24:9). These are the precise words spoken by Jacob as he blessed Judah, as recorded in Genesis 49:9. Jacob's words describe the fact that the Messiah would come from the tribe of Judah. The Messiah would be known as the Lion of the tribe of Judah. After conquering His foe, He would lie down and no one would dare rouse Him.

A Star Out of Jacob and a Scepter Out of Israel

Balak the king of the Moabites was angry with Balaam for failing to curse the Israelites. Whenever Balaam opened his mouth, out came words of blessing for Israel, and the prophecies were becoming increasingly specific as it relates to Israel's victory over their enemies by means of a conquering King. So Balak struck his hands together and said to Balaam, "I called you to curse my enemies, and look, you have bountifully blessed them these three times! Now therefore, flee to your place. I said I would greatly honor you, but in fact, the LORD has kept you back from honor" (Numbers 24:10-11). Balaam answered, "Did I not also speak to your messengers whom you sent to me, saying, 'If Balak were to give me his house full of silver and gold, I could not go beyond the word of the LORD, to do good or bad on my own will. What the LORD says, that I must speak'? And now, indeed, I am going to my people. Come, I will advise you what this people will do to your people in the latter days" (Numbers 24:12-14).

At this point, Balaam delivered his fourth oracle, a prophecy of great significance for the future of Israel and for the Messiah who would come out of Jacob. Here are Balaam's immortal words: "The utterance of Balaam the son of Beor, and the utterance of the man whose eyes are opened; the utterance of him who hears the words of God, and has the knowledge of the Most High, who sees the vision of the Almighty, who falls down, with eyes wide open: I see Him, but not now; I behold Him, but not near; a Star shall come out of Jacob; a Scepter shall rise out of Israel, and batter the brow of Moab, and destroy all the sons of tumult. And Edom shall be a possession; Seir also, his enemies, shall be a possession, while Israel does valiantly, out of Jacob One shall have dominion, and destroy the remains of the city" (Numbers 24:15-19).

When Balaam said that his eyes were opened he meant he understood what was he was saying. When he said, "I see Him, but not now; I behold Him, but not near," Balaam meant he could see prophetically into the future; he knew the Messiah would come, but many years would pass before this event. When Balaam said a Star would come out of Jacob and a Scepter out of Israel, he connected with two major points of messianic prophecy. First, Jacob had declared to his son Judah, "The scepter shall not depart from Judah, nor a lawgiver from between his feet, until Shiloh comes; and to Him shall be the obedience of the people" (Genesis 49:10). This means that Israel's king would be from the tribe of Judah. The untranslated Hebrew word *Shiloh* means "he to whom it belongs." The word anticipates the Messiah, who would be from the tribe of Judah and to whom the king's scepter belonged. Jacob's words to Judah concerning a donkey and a colt were interpreted by Zechariah as a reference to the Messiah's entry into Jerusalem, as seen in Matthew 21. When Balaam said, "A Scepter shall rise out of Israel," he was saying precisely what Jacob had previously declared.

Balaam's statement that a Star would come out of Jacob is the first mention of the word "star" in the Bible. Since this is in the Book of Numbers, it is in the law. It is quite significant that in the last chapter of the Bible Jesus is recorded as saying, "I, Jesus, have sent My angel to testify to you these things in the churches. I am the Root and the Offspring of David, the Bright and Morning Star" (Revelation 22:16). Other than "Surely I am coming quickly" (Revelation 22:20), these are the final recorded words of Jesus. In one of the earliest messianic prophecies, the Messiah is identified as a Star that rises out of Jacob, a prophecy that reaches all the way to the last book, the last chapter, and almost the last words of Jesus.

A Prophecy for the Church

Balaam prophesied this Star out of Jacob, this Scepter out of Israel, would possess Edom.[28] Many years later, the prophet Amos wrote, "On that day I will raise up the tabernacle of David, which has fallen down, and repair its damages; I will raise up its ruins, and rebuild it as in the days of old; that they may possess the remnant of Edom, and all the Gentiles who are called by My name, says the LORD who does this thing" (Amos 9:11-12). This reference to the restoration of the tabernacle of David has to do with the house of David, or with the Davidic throne, which was vacant after Coniah's rejection by God. The day would come, according to Amos, when the throne of David would again be occupied so Balaam's prophecy could be fulfilled. But we should notice that immediately after his reference to Edom, Amos continued with the words "and all the Gentiles who are called by My name." The Edomites were Gentiles, and it is of particular interest that the Hebrew word translated *Edom* could equally well be translated "mankind." The word *Edom* consists of precisely the same consonants as the word *Adam*, whose name means something like "earthling," representing all human beings, not just the Israelites. The original Hebrew language had no vowel markings, only consonants, so the word could be understood as a reference only to Edom or

84

to all human beings.

It is significant that Amos included the words "all the Gentiles" in view of the way the prophecy of Amos was used by James at the first church council, which met in 50 AD. At this council—the events of which are recorded in Acts 15—the apostles and elders were discussing whether Gentiles should be required to keep the law of Moses to be saved.[29] After Peter, Barnabas, and Paul had explained how God had saved Gentiles, making no distinction between them and the Jewish believers and purifying their hearts by faith, James said, "Men and brethren, listen to me: Simon has declared how God at the first visited the Gentiles to take out of them a people for His name. And with this the words of the prophets agree, just as it is written: 'After this I will return and will rebuild the tabernacle of David, which has fallen down; I will rebuild its ruins, and I will set it up; so that the rest of mankind may seek the LORD, even all the Gentiles who are called by My name, says the LORD who does all these things'" (Acts 15:13-16).

Based on the prophecy of Amos, James determined Gentile believers should not be required to keep the law of Moses. God had already saved them, even though they did not keep the law, and Amos had in fact prophesied this would happen. James understood the words of Amos in terms of the Messiah, Jesus Christ. With the coming of Christ, who was the descendant of David, the house of David was restored. This meant all human beings, not just the Israelites, could seek the LORD and be called by His name. This wonderful truth was foretold by Amos, but it was in fact anticipated long before Amos, by Balaam, the mercenary prophet, who saw the Messiah from afar, describing Him as a Star out of Jacob and a Scepter out of Israel who would, among other things, possess Edom— or in other words—who would be the God of all Gentiles who are called by His name. Today all Gentiles who are called by the name of Jesus are included in that ancient prophecy.

It is quite interesting to note that James, who made the connection between the prophecy of Amos and the inclusion of Gentiles in the church, warned early Christians about those who "blaspheme that noble name by which you are called" (James 2:7). Some students of Scripture recognize this is a reference to baptism in the Messiah's name. For example, the Amplified Bible translates James 2:7 this way: "Is it not they who slander and blaspheme that precious name by which you are distinguished and called [the name of Christ invoked in baptism]?"

When Jesus said all things that were written concerning Him in the Law must be fulfilled, it included even the prophecies of Balaam, whose motives were less than perfect, but who found himself unable to speak anything other than the words God put in his mouth.

6

The Prophet Like Moses

As he looked toward the future, Moses said to the ancient Israelites, "The LORD your God will raise up for you a Prophet like me from your midst, from your brethren. Him you shall hear, according to all you desired of the LORD your God in Horeb in the day of the assembly, saying, 'Let me not hear again the voice of the LORD my God, nor let me see this great fire anymore, lest I die.' And the LORD said to me: 'What they have spoken is good. I will raise up for them a Prophet like you from among their brethren, and will put My words in His mouth, and He shall speak to them all that I command Him. And it shall be that whoever will not hear My words, which He speaks in My name, I will require it of him'" (Deuteronomy 18:15-19).

Moses' words certainly give us an opportunity to further explore the idea of intertextuality, for we will see references to them in the Gospels and even in the Book of Acts. But if we read Genesis, Exodus, Leviticus, Numbers, and Deuteronomy as one book—an idea that arises from Scripture itself in references to the law, the law of Moses, and the Book of the Law—Moses' words will also give us an opportunity to explore innertextuality.

Let Not God Speak with Us

First, notice that Moses, in this prophecy, referred back to something the Israelites had said earlier. In the giving of the Ten Commandments, "the people witnessed the thunderings, the lightning flashes, the sound of the trumpet, and the mountain smoking; and when the people saw it, they trembled and stood afar off. Then they said to Moses, 'You speak with us, and we will hear; but let not God speak with us, lest we die'" (Exodus 20:18-19). This event was of such significance in the history of Israel that it is referred to in the New Testament in the letter to the Hebrews. In contrast to the law of Moses, the writer of Hebrews said, "For you have not come to the mountain that may be touched and that burned with fire, and to blackness and darkness and tempest, and the sound of a trumpet and the voice of words, so that those who heard it begged that the word should not be spoken to them anymore" (Hebrews 12:18-19).

We should take a moment and look at Moses' prophecy more carefully. First, when Moses said, "The LORD your God will raise up for you a Prophet like me," he anticipated a future for Israel. Moses would not be the final prophet. Another prophet like Moses would come. Second, when Moses said this prophet would be "from your midst, from your brethren," he indicated that the coming prophet would be an Israelite. At this point, it may seem superfluous to say that the coming prophet would be a human being, but we will note later that this is an important point in the prophecy. Third, the people of Israel were to hear or listen to this prophet because he would speak the words of God. Fourth, God would call to account anyone who refused to listen to this prophet's words.

Who Is the Prophet Like Moses?

Who would this prophet be? Since the Book of Joshua follows Deuteronomy, we may think that Joshua is the promised prophet. But the conclusion of Deuteronomy lets us know that this is not the case. It reads, "Now Joshua ... was full of the spirit of wisdom, for Moses had laid his hands on him; so the children of Israel heeded him, and did as the LORD had commanded Moses. But since then there has not arisen in Israel a prophet like Moses, whom the LORD knew face to face, in all the signs and wonders which the LORD sent him to do in the land of Egypt, before Pharaoh, before all his servants, and in all his land, and by all that mighty power and all the great terror which Moses performed in the sight of all Israel" (Deuteronomy 34:9-12). According to this text, although Joshua was full of the spirit of wisdom, he was not the prophet Moses had in mind, nor was Moses' prophecy fulfilled by any other prophet that arose in Israel up to the time these words were written. Also these final words of Deuteronomy suggest the prophet like Moses would be one whose ministry would be characterized by mighty signs and wonders like those of Moses when the LORD sent him to Pharaoh in Egypt.

On the basis of Moses' prophecy about another prophet like him, the ancient Israelites continued to look for that prophet. When John the Baptist came on the scene, some thought that he might be the prophet Moses foretold. When priests and Levites sent by the religious leaders in Jerusalem asked John, "Who are you?" John answered, "I am not the Christ," or the Messiah. Then they asked, "What then? Are you Elijah?" He said, "I am not." Next, they asked, "Are you the Prophet?" John said, "No."[30] John's questioners, who were from the Pharisees, inquired further. They said, "Why then do you baptize if you are not the Christ, nor Elijah, nor the Prophet?" (John 1:25). These questions indicate the prophet promised by Moses had not yet arrived, but his identity was of keen interest to the Jewish people.

Later after Jesus miraculously multiplied the loaves and fish to feed the five thousand, those who saw this sign said, "This is truly the Prophet who is to come into the world" (John 6:14). The very next verse reads, "Therefore when Jesus perceived that they were about to come and take Him by force to make Him king, He departed again to the mountain by Himself alone" (John 6:15). Apparently at this time in Jewish history, there was a connection in the minds of the people between the prophet promised by Moses and King Messiah. They expected this prophet to be their king.

The importance of Moses' prophecy can also be seen in its use by Stephen in defense of his faith. In his reference to Moses, Stephen said, "This is that Moses who said to the children of Israel, 'The LORD your God will raise up for you a Prophet like me from your brethren. Him you shall hear'" (Acts 7:37).

Jesus Is the Prophet Like Moses

But we finally learn the identity of the promised Prophet in the apostle Peter's words to those who gathered in Solomon's porch after the healing of the lame man at the Beautiful Gate of the Temple. Peter said, "Repent therefore and be converted, that your sins may be blotted out, so that times of refreshing may come from the presence of the Lord, and that He may send Jesus Christ, who was preached to you before, whom heaven must receive until the times of restoration of all things, which God has spoken by the mouth of all His holy prophets since the world began. For Moses truly said to the fathers, 'The LORD your God will raise up for you a Prophet like me from your brethren. Him you shall hear in all things, whatever He says to you. And it shall be that every soul who will not hear that Prophet shall be utterly destroyed from among the people.' Yes, and all the prophets, from Samuel and those who follow, as many as have spoken, have also foretold these days" (Acts 3:19-24). Peter quoted Moses' prophecy about a Prophet to come in such as way as to indicate that Jesus is that promised Prophet. And not only is Jesus the promised Prophet, He is also the seed promised to Abraham. Notice Peter's final words to the amazed multitude: "You are the sons of the prophets, and of the covenant which God made with our fathers, saying to Abraham, 'And in your seed all the families of the earth shall be blessed.' To you first, God, having raised up His Servant Jesus, sent Him to bless you, in turning away every one of you from your iniquities" (Acts 3:25-26).

Peter's identification of Jesus as the Prophet like Moses is the basis upon which he called for the people to repent and be converted in order to obtain the blotting out of their sins. Their conversion would also open the way for the times of refreshing to come from the presence of the Lord. This refreshing or renewal would involve the second coming of Jesus Christ, at which time everything would be restored that the Hebrew prophets had foretold.

We should also note that, after quoting Moses' prophecy, Peter said that all of the prophets had foretold "these days," that is, the events of the first century that were connected with the coming of Jesus. Later, as he met with Gentiles at the house of Cornelius to preach Christ to them, Peter said, "To Him all the prophets witness that, through His name, whoever believes in Him will receive remission of sin" (Acts 10:43).

The coherence of Peter's ministry in the Book of Acts is quite remarkable. He consistently declared that Jesus was the fulfillment of the messianic prophecies of the Hebrew Scriptures, drawing from such diverse Old Testament texts as Joel, Psalms, Genesis, and Deuteronomy. He also consistently called his hearers to repentance and water baptism, with the idea that baptism in the name of the Messiah, Jesus Christ, fulfilled the prophetic expectation that believers would both call upon the name of the Lord and be called by the name of the Lord. Peter connected repentance and water baptism with the remission, or forgiveness, or blotting out of sins. In his response to those who heard his initial proclamation of the gospel on the Day of Pentecost and who asked, "What shall we do?" Peter said, "Repent, and let every one of you be baptized in the name of Jesus Christ for the remission of sins; and you shall receive the gift of the Holy Spirit" (Acts 2:38). To the amazed crowd who gathered following the healing of the lame man at the Beautiful Gate, Peter said, "Repent therefore and be converted, that your sins may be blotted out" (Acts 3:19). To Simon the Sorcerer, who thought he could buy with money the ability to grant the gift of the Holy Spirit, Peter said, "Repent therefore of this your wickedness, and pray God if perhaps the thought of your heart may be forgiven you" (Acts 8:22). Then, to those gathered in the house of Cornelius, Peter declared, "To Him all the prophets witness that, through His name, whoever believes in Him will receive remission of sins" (Acts 10:43). In this case, the Holy Spirit fell upon everyone who heard the word. The Jewish believers who had accompanied Peter to the house of Cornelius, a Gentile, were astonished when they heard the Gentiles speaking miraculously in languages they had never learned, just as the Jewish believers had done on the Day of Pentecost. But still, even though these people had already been filled with the Holy Spirit, Peter did not neglect to emphasize the importance of water baptism. He asked, "Can anyone forbid water, that these should not be baptized who have received the Holy Spirit just as we have?" (Acts 10:47). Then, Peter "commanded them to be baptized in the name of the Lord" (Acts 10:48). The earliest Greek manuscripts tell us that Peter commanded the people at Cornelius's house to be baptized in the name of Jesus Christ.

Stop and think for a moment. It is a bold and radical thing for anyone to presume to tell another person what to do in order to obtain forgiveness of sins. The reason Peter was willing to tell people that forgiveness was linked to believing on Jesus, repenting of their sins, and being baptized in the name of Jesus Christ, is that he was convinced that Jesus fulfilled all of the prophecies of the coming Messiah, the seed of the woman, the seed of Abraham, the prophet like Moses, and the seed of David. Peter knew Moses had said, "And it shall be that every soul who will not hear that Prophet shall be utterly destroyed from among the people" (Acts 3:23). Biblically, to hear includes the idea of obedience.

Four Aspects of Moses' Prophecy

Moses' prophecy of a coming Prophet like him, which may at first seem merely to be an obscure Old Testament text, turns out to be one of the most profound and influential messianic prophecies in the Hebrew Scriptures, referred to again and again and finding its fulfillment in the person of Jesus Christ. Now that we know this, it will be helpful to look closely at the prophecy once more. We noticed that when Moses said, "The LORD your God will raise up for you a Prophet like me," he anticipated a future for Israel. Moses would not be the final prophet. Another prophet like Moses would come. Although the nation of Israel suffered deep spiritual and political crises, including the destruction of the city of Jerusalem, the desecration of Solomon's Temple, and captivity in Assyria and Babylon, Moses' promise was still good well over one thousand years after he spoke those words.

Second, Moses said this Prophet would be "from your midst, from your brethren," indicating the coming prophet would be an Israelite. Although Jesus Christ is God, He is God manifest in human existence. Specifically, He is God manifest as a descendant of the people of Israel, the tribe of Judah, and the house of David.

Third, the people of Israel were to hear or listen to this Prophet because he would speak the words of God. Jesus said, "The words that I speak to you are spirit, and they are life" (John 6:63).

Fourth, God would call to account anyone who refused to listen to this Prophet's words. Jesus said, "If anyone hears My words and does not believe, I do not judge him; for I did not come to judge the world but to save the world. He who rejects Me, and does not receive My words, has that which judges him—the word that I have spoken will judge him in the last day. For I have not spoken on My own authority; but the Father who sent Me gave Me a command, what I should say and what I should speak. And I know that His command is everlasting life. Therefore, whatever I speak, just as the Father has told me, so I speak" (John 12:47-50).

The Messiah's Name in the Hebrew Scriptures

On another note, it is interesting to see how the Messiah's name is found at the seams of the Old Testament. When we say "the seams," we mean where the Law meets the Prophets and where the Prophets meet the Psalms. Jesus said everything written concerning Him in the Law, the Prophets, and the Psalms must be fulfilled.[31] To see this important point, we must recognize that the name "Jesus" is the English transliteration of the Greek *Iesous*. *Iesous* is the Greek transliteration of the Hebrew *Yeshua`*, commonly transliterated in the Old Testament as Joshua. In other words, Joshua and Jesus are the same name, with the same meaning. Depending on the context in which the name is used, it could be translated "Yahweh-Savior," "Yahweh will save," or "Yahweh is Salvation." In many English translations, the name "Yahweh," by which God revealed Himself to Moses, is rendered as "Jehovah."

Even though Joshua, who followed Moses as the

leader of Israel, was not the promised Prophet, it seems prophetically significant that Moses' immediate successor had the same name as the promised Prophet. The very next book after the close of the Law, the first book of the Prophets, carries the name of the promised Prophet. It is Joshua.

Next, if we read the Book of Zechariah, we discover another Joshua who, despite the strict separation between the priesthood and the royal throne in the law of Moses, is both a king and priest. Zechariah wrote, "Take the silver and gold, make an elaborate crown, and set it on the head of Joshua the son of Jehozadak, the high priest. Then speak to him, saying, 'Thus says the LORD of hosts, saying, "Behold, the Man whose name is the BRANCH! From His place He shall branch out, and He shall build the temple of the LORD; yes, He shall build the temple of the LORD. He shall bear the glory, and shall sit and rule on His throne; so He shall be a priest on His throne, and the counsel of peace shall be between them both"'" (Zechariah 6:11-13). This Joshua, a priest, will also sit and rule on His throne. This anticipated a day when the law of Moses would no longer be in effect. Under the law, a priest could not rule on Israel's throne, nor could a king function in the office of the priesthood. But when this priest is on His throne, there will be "a counsel of peace" between the priesthood and royalty.

This Joshua, who is identified as the BRANCH, represents the Branch who grows from the stem of Jesse, according to Isaiah 11:1. In other words, He is from the house of David and sits on the throne of David. Thus He is not from the tribe of Levi and cannot serve as a priest under the law of Moses. Instead He is a priest forever according to the order of Melchizedek (Hebrews 5:6). This identification of the Messiah is rooted in the psalm most frequently quoted in the New Testament. Psalm 110:4 reads, "The LORD has sworn and will not relent, You are a priest forever according to the order of Melchizedek." Jesus Himself declared Psalm 110 to be about the Messiah when He quoted the first verse to confound the unbelieving Pharisees: "The LORD said to my Lord, 'Sit at My right hand, till I make Your enemies Your footstool.'"

How can we say the Joshua of the Book of Zechariah represents the Messiah in such a way that the Messiah's name appears at the seam between the Prophets and the Psalms? The Book of Zechariah is one of the books often identified as the twelve Minor Prophets. They are found at the end of our English translations. But for the ancient Hebrews, these books actually formed one book, the Book of the Twelve. They were, in other words, considered one book with twelve authors. Then, in the Hebrew order of the books that we call the Old Testament, an order used by Jesus when He referred to the Law, the Prophets, and the Psalms, the Book of the Twelve is the last book at the end of the section identified as the Prophets. The next book, following the Book of the Twelve, is Psalms. So not only does the name "Joshua" have a high profile where the Law meets the Prophets, it also is placed significantly where the Prophets meet the Psalms. The significance of this may be seen further by comparing Joshua 1 with Psalm 1. Joshua 1:8 reads, "This Book of the Law shall not depart from your mouth, but you shall meditate in it day and night, that you may observe to do according to all that is written in it. For then you will make your way prosperous, and then you will have good success." Psalm

1:2-3 read, "But his delight is in the law of the LORD, and in His law he meditates day and night. He shall be like a tree planted by the rivers of water, that brings forth its fruit in its season, whose leaf also shall not wither; and whatever he does shall prosper."

The Prophet promised by Moses has come. His name is Jesus. Although He is God, He is—by means of the miracle of the Incarnation—also one of us. He speaks to us the Word of God, and it is essential to our spiritual well-being that we hear Him.

PART II

How the Prophets Reveal Jesus

7

The Davidic Covenant

Jesus said everything written concerning Him in the Law of Moses, the Prophets, and the Psalms must be fulfilled.[32] This is a reference to the three sections of the Hebrew Scriptures. We have discussed some of the references to the Messiah in the Law; now we will turn our attention to some of those things said about Him in the Prophets. We are doing this in order to grow in knowledge of our Lord and Savior, Jesus Christ.[33]

To the amazed onlookers who gathered in Solomon's Porch following the healing of the lame man at the Beautiful Gate, Peter said, "All the prophets, from Samuel and those who follow, as many as have spoken, have also foretold these days" (Acts 3:24). When he said "these days," Peter meant the days that began with the coming of Jesus Christ.[34] Since Peter specifically referred to the prophet Samuel and all who followed Samuel, we should note that according to the order in which the books are found in the Hebrew Scriptures, this means that the following books foretold events associated with the coming of the Messiah: I and II Samuel, I and II Kings, Isaiah, Jeremiah, Ezekiel, Hosea, Joel, Amos, Obadiah, Jonah, Micah, Nahum, Habakkuk, Zephaniah, Haggai, Zechariah, and Malachi.[35] We will begin with Samuel's prophetic statements concerning the Messiah.

Messianic Prophecy in II Samuel

The Book of II Samuel records David's interest in building a house for the Lord. David said to the prophet Nathan, "See now, I dwell in a house of cedar, but the ark of God dwells inside tent curtains" (II Samuel 7:2). At first, Nathan said, "Go, do all that is in your heart, for the LORD is with you" (II Samuel 7:3). That night, however, the word of the LORD came to Nathan. The essence of the message was that instead of David building a house for the LORD, the LORD would build a house for David: "Also the LORD tells you that He will make you a house. When your days are fulfilled and you rest with your fathers, I will set up your seed after you, who will come from your body, and I will establish his kingdom. He shall build a house for My name, and I will establish the throne of his kingdom forever. I will be his Father, and he shall be My son. If he commits iniquity, I will chasten him with the rod of men and with the blows of the sons of men. But My mercy shall not depart from him, as I took it from Saul, whom I removed from before you. And your house and your kingdom shall be established forever before you. Your throne shall be established forever" (II Samuel 7:11b-16).

After Nathan reported these words to David, David prayed a prayer of thanksgiving, focusing on the promise of the longevity of his throne. David prayed, "You have ... spoken of Your servant's house for a great while to come. ...

establish it forever and do as You have said.... let it please You to bless the house of Your servant, that it may continue before You forever; for You, O Lord GOD, have spoken it, and with Your blessing let the house of Your servant be blessed forever" (II Samuel 7:19, 25, 29).

An inspired reflection on the permanence of this covenant can be seen in the contemplation of Ethan the Ezrahite, found in Psalm 89. In part, Ethan wrote, "I have made a covenant with My chosen, I have sworn to My servant David: 'Your seed I will establish forever, and build up your throne to all generations.' ... My mercy I will keep for him forever, and My covenant shall stand firm with him. His seed also I will make to endure forever, and his throne as the days of heaven. ... My covenant I will not break, nor alter the word that has gone out of My lips. Once I have sworn by My holiness; I will not lie to David: his seed shall endure forever, and his throne as the sun before Me; it shall be established forever like the moon, even like the faithful witness in the sky" (Psalm 89:3-4, 28-29, 34-37). But at the time Ethan wrote, after the death of David and apparently after the death of Solomon, when the kingdom was in disarray and divided between Israel in the north and Judah in the south, it seemed to Ethan that God had renounced His covenant with David. Verses 38-51 of Psalm 89 sound a note of despair at the apparent disintegration of the Davidic Covenant. But at the very end of the Psalm, and thus at the end of Book Three of the Psalter, there is a glimmer of hope once again in the words, "Blessed be the LORD forevermore! Amen and Amen" (Psalm 89:52).

We may think because of the statement, "If he commits iniquity, I will chasten him with the rod of men and with the blows of the sons of men,"—an idea reiterated in Psalm 89:30-32—that this prophecy was fulfilled by Solomon or by subsequent descendants from David. But although they were included in the range of this prophetic promise, Solomon and other descendants of David who ruled on the temporal throne of the house of David did not exhaust the meaning of this prophecy. The prophecy looked far beyond David's merely human descendants to One who, although physically descended from David, would also, by means of the Incarnation, be the Son of God Himself.

Gabriel and the Davidic Covenant

About a thousand years after God made this promise to David, the angel Gabriel appeared to the virgin Mary, who was a physical descendant of David, with the good news that she was highly favored and blessed among women and that the Lord was with her. She was troubled at this news, but Gabriel continued, "Do not be afraid, Mary, for you have found favor with God. And behold, you will conceive in your womb and bring forth a Son, and shall call His name JESUS. He will be great, and will be called the Son of the Highest; and the Lord God will give Him the throne of His father David. And He will reign over the house of Jacob forever, and of His kingdom there will be no end" (Luke 1:30-33). Gabriel's words are a virtual quote from II Samuel 7:16. God had said to David that his *house* and *kingdom* and *throne* would be established forever. Gabriel said to Mary that the Lord God would give her son, Jesus, the *throne* of His father David, that He would reign over the *house* of Jacob forever, and that there would be no end of his *kingdom.* This is a splendid example of intertextuality in Scripture. Gabriel's words serve to interpret the ultimate and final meaning of the Davidic Covenant. The covenant finds its fulfillment in the Messiah, Jesus Christ, who is David's greatest Son. But He is, at the same time, the Son of God, because the conception in Mary's womb would be due to the miraculous work of the Holy Spirit. Mary did not understand how this could be, but Gabriel explained that "with God nothing will be impossible" (Luke 1:37).

Zacharias and the Davidic Covenant

When Zacharias, the father of John the Baptist, was filled with the Holy Spirit he uttered a prophecy linking John's ministry as the forerunner of the Messiah with the ancient prophecy Nathan made to David. Zacharias said, "Blessed is the Lord God of Israel, for He has visited and redeemed His people, and has raised up a horn of salvation for us in the house of His servant David, as He spoke by the mouth of His holy prophets, who have been since the world began" (Luke 1:68-70).

Peter and the Davidic Covenant

The Davidic Covenant was a central feature of the apostle Peter's message on the Day of Pentecost. Peter quoted the following words from Psalm 16:8-11, identifying them as the words of the Messiah: "I foresaw the Lord always before my face, for He is at my right hand, that I may not be shaken. Therefore my heart rejoiced, and my tongue was glad; moreover my flesh also will rest in hope. For You will not leave my soul in Hades, nor will You allow Your Holy One to see corruption. You have made known to me the ways of life; You will make me full

105

of joy in Your presence" (Acts 2:25-28). We may at first think these are the words of David about his own situation, but Peter explained that this is not the case. Instead, he continued, "Men and brethren, let me speak freely to you of the patriarch David, that he is both dead and buried, and his tomb is with us to this day. Therefore, being a prophet, and knowing that God had sworn with an oath to him that of the fruit of his body, according to the flesh, He would raise up the Christ to sit on his throne, he, foreseeing this, spoke concerning the resurrection of Christ, that His soul was not left in Hades, nor did His flesh see corruption. This Jesus God has raised up, of which we are all witnesses" (Acts 2:29-32). According to Peter, David was a prophet who knew God's oath to him meant the Messiah would be his physical descendant. Not only that, but David understood that Christ, the Messiah, would sit on his throne following the Messiah's resurrection from the dead, a resurrection that would occur before He had been dead long enough for His flesh to corrupt. Peter also apparently saw a connection between the prophetic significance of the throne of David and the post-resurrection ascension of Christ, for he continued: 'This Jesus God has raised up, of which we are all witnesses. Therefore being exalted to the right hand of God, and having received from the Father the promise of the Holy Spirit, He poured out this which you now see and hear. For David did not ascend into the heavens, but he says himself: 'The Lord said to my Lord, sit at My right hand, till I make Your enemies Your footstool.' Therefore let all the house of Israel know assuredly that God has made this Jesus, whom you crucified, both Lord and Christ" (Acts 2:32-36).

How could it be that the prophetic throne of David is connected with the Messiah's exaltation to the right hand of God? If we keep in mind that David was a prophet who foresaw the death and resurrection of the Messiah, a Messiah who would be David's physical descendant, we can find clues to the answer in the Psalms. It will help us when we read the psalms to remember the Hebrew word often translated "Anointed" is *Mashiach*, from which comes the English "Messiah." In other words we can read the word "Anointed" as a reference to the Messiah. One example is found in Psalm 132:10-18: "For Your servant David's sake, do not turn away the face of Your Anointed. The LORD has sworn in truth to David; He will not turn from it: 'I will set upon your throne the fruit of your body. If your sons will keep My covenant and My testimony which I shall teach them, their sons also shall sit upon your throne forevermore.' For the LORD has chosen Zion; He has desired it for His dwelling place: 'This is My resting place forever; here I will dwell, for I have desired it. I will abundantly bless her provision; I will satisfy her poor with bread. I will also clothe her priests with salvation, and her saints shall shout aloud for joy. There I will make the horn of David grow; I will prepare a lamp for My Anointed. His enemies I will clothe with shame, but upon Himself His crown shall flourish."

Psalm 132 is structured in much the same way as II Samuel 7, where God established His covenant with David. II Samuel 7 begins with David's expression of his interest in building a dwelling place for the LORD. Psalm 132 begins with a reflection on David's desire to find a dwelling place for the LORD: "LORD, remember David and all his afflictions; how he swore to the LORD, and vowed to the

Mighty One of Jacob: 'Surely I will not go into the chamber of my house, or go up to the comfort of my bed; I will not give sleep to my eyes or slumber to my eyelids, until I find a place for the LORD, a dwelling place for the Mighty One of Jacob'" (Psalm 132:1-5). Just as II Samuel 7 goes on to detail the establishment of God's covenant with David, so Psalm 132 continues to describe the Davidic Covenant. But in Psalm 132, between the reflection on David's desire to find a dwelling place for the LORD and the reiteration of the Davidic Covenant, we discover these interesting words: "Behold, we heard of it in Ephrathah; We found it in the fields of the woods" (Psalm 132:6). What could this mean? Where is Ephrathah? What was found in the fields of the woods?

A Discovery in Ephrathah, in the
Fields of the Woods

In a very specific prophecy of the coming Messiah, the prophet Micah wrote, "But you, Bethlehem Ephrathah, though you are little among the thousands of Judah, yet out of you shall come forth to Me the One to be Ruler in Israel, whose goings forth are from of old, from everlasting" (Micah 5:2). This is, of course, a prophecy of the birth of the Messiah in Bethlehem. This is the prophecy to which the chief priests and scribes referred when Herod asked them where the Christ was to be born. His question was prompted by the arrival of wise men from the East who wished to locate and worship the recently born King of the Jews, whose star they had seen. The chief priests and scribes answered Herod, "In Bethlehem of Judea, for thus it is written by the prophet: 'But you, Bethlehem, in the land of Judah, are not the least among the rulers of Judah; for out of you shall come a Ruler who will shepherd My people Israel'" (Matthew 2:5-6).

Where is Ephrathah? Ephrathah is another name for Bethlehem. But what was heard of in Ephrathah? Who heard it? What was found in the fields of the woods? Who found it? On the night of Jesus' birth in Bethlehem, the city of David, "there were in the same country shepherds living out in the fields, keeping watch over their flock by night. And behold, an angel of the Lord stood before them, and the glory of the Lord shone around them, and they were greatly afraid. Then the angel said to them, 'Do not be afraid, for behold, I bring you good tidings of great joy which will be to all people. For there is born to you this day in the city of David a Savior, who is Christ the Lord. And this will be the sign to you: You will find a Babe wrapped in swaddling cloths, lying in a manger'" (Luke 2:8-12).

Although Psalm 132:6 may have referred to the ark of the covenant as the psalm was originally written before its inclusion in the Psalter, the contextual influence of the entire Book of Psalms suggests it should be read here as a bit of prophetic insight into the location of the permanent dwelling place of God in the Messiah Himself, Jesus, who was born in Bethlehem and whose birth was discovered by the shepherds of Bethlehem as it was announced to them by the angel as they were watching their flocks in the fields. This is further suggested by the shepherds' response to the angel's announcement. In Psalm 132, immediately after the reference to something being discovered in Ephrathah, in the fields of the woods, we find these words: "Let us go into His tabernacle; let us worship at His footstool" (Psalm 132:7). After the shepherds had heard the good news from the angels, they said to one another, "Let us now go to Bethlehem and see this thing that has come to pass, which the Lord has made known to us" (Luke 2:15). Even the shepherds' response after finding Mary and Joseph and the Babe lying in a manger is remarkably similar to the words found in Psalm 132:9: "Let Your priests be clothed with righteousness, and let Your saints shout for joy." Luke records that "the shepherds returned, glorifying and praising God for all the things that they heard and seen, as it was told them" (Luke 2:20).

The Throne of David and the Right Hand of God

Now let's return to our question, "How could it be that the prophetic throne of David is connected with the Messiah's exaltation to the right hand of God?" David's throne was set up in Zion, the location of Jerusalem. After reiterating the content of the Davidic Covenant, including the fact that the Messiah would be a physical descendant of David who would sit on David's throne, Psalm 132 continues, "For the LORD has chosen Zion; He has desired it for His dwelling place: 'This is My resting place forever; here I will dwell, for I have desired it. ... There I will make the horn of David grow; I will prepare a lamp for My Anointed. His enemies I will clothe with shame, but upon Himself His crown shall flourish" (Psalm 132:13-14, 17-18).

Although the Hebrew Scriptures anticipate the restoration of Israel to the land promised to Abraham, Isaac, and Jacob, in a time of peace and security, and in an era featuring the restoration of the Davidic throne,[36] they also foretell a time when the heavens and the earth will perish.

This prophecy is found in Psalm 102:25-27: "Of old You laid the foundation of the earth, and the heavens are the work of Your hands. They will perish, but You will endure; yes, they will grow old like a garment; like a cloak You will change them, and they will be changed. But You are the same, and Your years will have no end." The apostle Peter explained it this way: "But the day of the Lord will come as a thief in the night, in which the heavens will pass away with a great noise, and the elements will melt with fervent heat; both the earth and the works that are in it will be burned up. Therefore, since all these things will be dissolved, what manner of persons ought you to be in holy conduct and godliness, looking for and hastening the coming of the day of God, because of which the heavens will be dissolved, being on fire, and the elements will melt with fervent heat? Nevertheless we, according to His promise, look for new heavens and a new earth in which righteousness dwells" (II Peter 3:10-13).

How can the Davidic Covenant be an everlasting covenant, with the Messiah ruling on the throne of David forever in the city of Jerusalem, if the entire earth will be destroyed? The answer is found when we turn to the closing chapters of the Bible's final book, Revelation. There we read these words of John: "Now I saw a new heaven and a new earth, for the first heaven and the first earth had passed away. Also there was no more sea. Then I, John, saw the holy city, New Jerusalem, coming down out of heaven from God, prepared as a bride adorned for her husband. And I heard a loud voice from heaven saying, 'Behold, the tabernacle of God is with men, and He will dwell with them, and they shall be His people. God Himself will be with them and be their God'" (Revelation 21:1-3).

This New Jerusalem has no temple, because the Lamb, who is the Lord God Almighty, is its temple.[37] But it does have a throne, and the Lamb sits on the throne. The Lamb is, of course, Jesus Christ, who was identified by John the Baptist as the Lamb of God that takes away the sin of the world. Because the throne in the New Jerusalem is occupied by Jesus Christ, it becomes the ultimate and final throne of David, eternally fulfilling the Davidic Covenant. We know this because Jesus Himself says, in some of His last words recorded in Scripture, "I, Jesus, have sent My angel to testify to you these things in the churches. I am the Root and the Offspring of David, the Bright and Morning Star" (Revelation 22:16).

Upon whatever throne the Offspring of David sits is the throne of David. There would otherwise have been no reason for Jesus to identify Himself as David's descendant. Thus we find the remarkable fulfillment of Nathan's prophecy as it was recorded in II Samuel 7, and we find the accuracy of Peter's statement that all of the prophets, from Samuel and those who follow, foretold the days of Jesus the Messiah.

8

A Son Is Given

In the eighth century BC, a Hebrew prophet named Isaiah uttered startling and specific prophecies to his people. In the days before the invasion of Jerusalem by Babylon, most of the people of Judah were in such flagrant violation of God's laws that Isaiah compared them to Sodom and Gomorrah.[38] Isaiah was quite clear in his prediction that God would use foreign oppressors to judge His people. This would result in captivity in Assyria for the northern kingdom of Israel in 722 BC and captivity in Babylon for the southern kingdom of Judah in 586 BC.

Swords into Plowshares; Spears into Pruning Hooks

But threaded throughout Isaiah's identification of the sins of the people are wonderful prophecies of a day when their sins would be forgiven, they would be restored to fellowship with God, and all of the promises God had made with their ancestors would be fulfilled. For example, Isaiah's prophecy of a bright future for Judah and Jerusalem is found in the second chapter of the book: "Now it shall come to pass in the latter days that the mountain of the LORD's house shall be established on the top of the mountains, and shall be exalted above the hills; and all nations shall flow to it. Many people shall come and say, 'Come, and let us go up to the mountain of the LORD, to the house of the God of Jacob; He will teach us His ways, and we shall walk in His paths.' For out of Zion shall go forth the law, and the word of the LORD from Jerusalem. He shall judge between the nations, and rebuke many people; they shall beat their swords into plowshares, and their spears into pruning hooks; nation shall not lift up sword against nation, neither shall they learn war anymore" (Isaiah 2:2-4).

As we shall see, some of Isaiah's prophecies have already been fulfilled. Some of them were fulfilled long ago. But some still await fulfillment, such as the prophecy we just read. We have yet to see the construction of the LORD's house in Mount Zion as described in this prophecy. Although a second temple was built after the Babylonian exile in an attempt to recapture the glory of Solomon's Temple, this second temple was so inferior to the magnificent structure built by Solomon that the old men, who had seen the first temple, wept even when they saw the limited dimensions of its foundation.[39] This second temple was not the LORD's house foretold by Isaiah. When this house is built, it will be a center of worship for people all over the world. All nations will flow to it. This means it will attract Gentile as well as Jewish worshipers. At that time, war will be a thing of the past. The instruments of war will be refashioned into agricultural implements.

We may be tempted to interpret a prophecy like this allegorically or symbolically. But the fact that so many of Isaiah's prophecies have already been fulfilled literally indicates we should expect all of them to have a literal fulfillment. To anticipate a literal fulfillment of prophecies like these can give us great joy, for they offer hope in the face of worldwide violence and ongoing warfare that things will not always be this way. The day will come when there will be no further military or social tension, even in the Middle East. The precise geographical location that has been the flash point for deadly friction for century after century of human history will one day be the center of peaceful reconciliation for all nations of the world, as they say, "Come, and let us go up to the mountain of the LORD, to the house of the God of Jacob; He will teach us His ways, and we shall walk in His paths" (Isaiah 2:3).

The Branch of the Lord

In the fourth chapter of Isaiah another prophecy is found: "In that day the Branch of the LORD shall be beautiful and glorious" (Isaiah 4:2). Later, in the eleventh chapter of the book, we discover the Branch is the Messiah, who comes forth from the stem or stock of Jesse, David's father.[40] The Spirit of the LORD rests upon Him, and He will introduce an era of peace that includes the removal of the enmity between the animal kingdom and human beings and is characterized by the earth being full of the knowledge of the LORD as the waters cover the sea. (See Isaiah 11:9.)

Isaiah's Vision

In the year that King Uzziah of Judah died, Isaiah had a vision in which he "saw the Lord sitting on a throne, high and lifted up, and the train of his robe filled the temple" (Isaiah 6:1). Flying seraphim cried to one another, "Holy, holy, holy is the LORD of hosts; the whole earth is full of His glory!" (Isaiah 6:3). The seraphim identified the Lord as Yahweh, using the covenant name by which God had revealed Himself to Moses.[41] If we read this story carefully, we note the Lord seen by Isaiah was none other than the Messiah. We know this because the Lord is sitting on His throne, but the train of His robe fills the Temple. It is in the Messiah the throne and the Temple are brought together, because He is both King and Priest. The identity of the Lord as Messiah is confirmed by John, who explained why many did not believe on Jesus even though He had done so many miraculous signs before them.[42] John wrote, "Therefore they could not believe, because Isaiah said again: 'He has blinded their eyes and hardened their hearts, lest they should see with their eyes, lest they should understand with their hearts and turn, so that I should heal them'" (John 12:39-40). By this reference to Isaiah 6:9-10, John indicated he understood Isaiah's vision to be of the Messiah, Jesus. We know this because immediately after his quote from Isaiah 6, John wrote, "These things Isaiah said when he saw His glory and spoke of Him" (John 12:41). Throughout this passage John spoke of Jesus. The context indicates Isaiah saw the glory of the Messiah and spoke of the Messiah. Isaiah, in full agreement with the seraphim, said, "My eyes have seen the King, the LORD of hosts" (Isaiah 6:5b).

The Virgin Shall Conceive

One of the most striking and specific prophecies of Isaiah is found in a message the prophet gave to Ahaz, the king of Judah. Ahaz faced a military threat from a coalition formed by the kings of Israel and Syria. The LORD told Isaiah to take his son with him and to meet Ahaz at the end of the aqueduct from the upper pool on the highway to the fuller's field (Isaiah 7:3). Isaiah was to say to Ahaz, "Take heed, and be quiet; do not fear or be fainthearted for these two stubs of smoking firebrands" who had said, "Let us go up against Judah and trouble it, and let us make a gap in its wall for ourselves, and set a king over them" (Isaiah 7:4, 6). The good news for Ahaz was that the plan of these kings would fail. It was the responsibility of Ahaz, however, to respond to Isaiah's words in faith. Isaiah said, "If you will not believe, surely you will not be established" (Isaiah 7:9b).

In order to encourage Ahaz to believe Isaiah's prophecy, the LORD told Ahaz, "Ask a sign for yourself from the LORD your God; ask it either in the depth or in the height above" (Isaiah 7:11). Here was a splendid opportunity for Ahaz to obtain divine confirmation of Isaiah's prophecy. He could request a supernatural event as assurance that Isaiah had accurately communicated the word of God to him. Instead, however, Ahaz, with a pretense of piety, said, "I will not ask, nor will I test the LORD!" (Isaiah 7:12).

We might think this would be the end of the matter; if Ahaz did not want a sign that God would deliver His people, surely God would not give one. It may seem reasonable to think that if Ahaz had no faith, God would give no sign. But that is not the case. Instead, the LORD said, through Isaiah, "Hear now, O house of David! Is it a small thing for you to weary men, but will you weary my God also? Therefore the Lord Himself will give you a sign: Behold, the virgin shall conceive and bear a Son, and shall call His name Immanuel" (Isaiah 7:13-14). Those who are familiar with the New Testament will immediately recognize these words; they are found in the first chapter of the first book of the New Testament, where their fulfillment is explained.

When Joseph discovered during the time of their betrothal that Mary was expecting a child, he assumed she had been unfaithful to him. He knew the law of Moses required her to be stoned, but he was a just man who did not want to make a public example of Mary, even if she had sinned.[43] The only thing Joseph could think to do was to divorce Mary secretly. But an angel of the Lord appeared to Joseph in a dream with this message: "Joseph, son of David, do not be afraid to take to you Mary your wife, for that which is conceived in her is of the Holy Spirit. And she will bring forth a Son, and you shall call His name JESUS, for He will save His people from their sins" (Matthew 1:20-21). Then, Matthew, who frequently identified events foretold by the Hebrew prophets, wrote, "So all this was done that it might be fulfilled which was spoken by the Lord through the prophet, saying: 'Behold, the virgin shall be with child, and bear a Son, and they shall call His name Immanuel,' which is translated, 'God with us'" (Matthew 1:22-23).

A Sign for the House of David

How could Matthew claim a prophecy given to Ahaz nearly eight hundred years earlier was fulfilled in the conception of Jesus in the womb of the virgin Mary? How could the birth of Jesus be a sign to Ahaz, who had been dead for centuries? Questions like these have caused some to deny the accuracy of Matthew's statement. But a closer look at Isaiah's prophecy removes this problem. Although it is true that God offered a personal sign to Ahaz, a sign that would be meaningful to him in connection with God's promise that Judah would not be conquered by the coalition between Israel and Syria, when Ahaz refused the offer, the LORD turned His attention from Ahaz as an individual to the house of David at large. This can be seen in that following the refusal of Ahaz to request a divine sign, the next words of the LORD are, "Hear now, O house of David!" (Isaiah 7:13). Ahaz was a descendant of David, but he was not the only descendant of David. The term "house of David" included all of David's descendants. The expansion of the promise beyond Ahaz is also seen in the statement, "Therefore the Lord Himself will give you a sign" (Isaiah 7:14). The Hebrew word translated "you" is plural, indicating that this sign is not for Ahaz alone; it is for the entire house of David. This sign is that a virgin would conceive and bear a Son; the Son's name would be called Immanuel, which, as Matthew pointed out, means "God with us."

Some who reject Matthew's interpretation of this prophecy point out that the Hebrew word *almah*, often translated "virgin," may refer simply to a young woman of marriageable age. But besides the fact that a young unmarried woman was assumed to be a virgin in ancient Israel, we would have to ask what kind of a sign it would be for a young woman to have a son. It is evident from the context in Isaiah that the sign is miraculous; it is not something so common as to happen daily and without divine intervention. In response to this objection, it is quite significant that when Matthew quoted Isaiah 7:14, he followed the Septuagint, a Greek translation of the Hebrew text which was translated in the third century BC and which is used in the majority of places where the New Testament quotes from the Old Testament. Since the New Testament is inspired equally with the Old Testament, we accept these quotations from the Septuagint as accurately representing the meaning of the Hebrew text. In the case of Isaiah 7:14, the Septuagint translates the Hebrew *almah* with the Greek *parthenos*, which focuses on virginity. As Matthew indicates, the fact that this Son would be conceived of a virgin makes this a truly miraculous sign. The Son was conceived of the Holy Spirit.

Another comparison of Isaiah 7 and Matthew 1 underscores the amazing detail of Isaiah's prophecy. In Isaiah, after Ahaz rejected God's offer of a personal supernatural sign, the LORD promised a sign to the entire house of David, or to David's descendants. In Matthew, the angel that appeared to Joseph in a dream said, "Joseph, son of David, do not be afraid to take to you Mary your wife, for that which is conceived in her is of the Holy Spirit" (Matthew 1:20). The fact that the angel identified Joseph as the son of David connects this event with Isaiah's prophecy to the house of David.

It is at least possible there is another connection between Isaiah 7 and Matthew 1. The LORD had offered Ahaz the opportunity to ask for a supernatural sign either in the depth or in the height above.[44] When Ahaz refused, the LORD announced that He would give a supernatural sign to the entire house of David. It turned out that this sign involved both the height above and the depth below. This sign would be the Incarnation, whereby God is manifest in human existence.[45] This sign involved both the height, in that God came down from the heavens, and the depth, in that He was manifest as a human being on the earth. Ahaz refused to ask for a sign either in heaven or on earth, but God gave a sign in both heaven and earth, bringing both together in a supernatural event that united God and man in a virgin's womb and that further united them in the salvation that would be provided by the virgin's Son, whose name would be called Jesus, which means "Yahweh-Savior." This meant far more than the mere deliverance of the people of Judah from the kings of Israel and Syria in the days of Ahaz; it meant this promised Son would save His people from their sins.

A Son Who Is the Everlasting Father

Isaiah 7 is not the only place in the book where we find a prophecy of a Son who would be of the house of David but who would be far more than a mere human. Isaiah also gave this startling prophecy: "For unto us a Child is born, unto us a Son is given; and the government will be upon His shoulder. And His name will be called Wonderful, Counselor, Mighty God, Everlasting Father, Prince of Peace. Of the increase of His government and peace there will be no end, upon the throne of David and over His kingdom, to order it and establish it with judgment and justice from that time forward, even forever. The zeal of the LORD of hosts will perform this" (Isaiah 9:6-7). When we read these words, we think immediately of Gabriel's announcement to Mary: "And behold, you will conceive in your womb and bring forth a Son, and shall call His name JESUS. He will be great, and will be called the Son of the Highest; and the Lord God will give Him the throne of His father David. And He will reign over the house of Jacob forever, and of His kingdom there will be no end" (Luke 1:31-33). In both Isaiah and Luke, a Son is in view. He is identified by a specific name. He is a descendant of David. He will rule on David's throne. His kingdom will endure forever.

Think for a moment about the significance of the name given to this Son in Isaiah and the name given in Luke. At this point it is important we understand the theology of name among the ancient Israelites. Contrary to the custom of some cultures whereby a child's name is viewed simply as a label by which the child is known, the ancient Hebrews viewed a name as so thoroughly descriptive of the identity of the person that it could be said in a very real sense that a person was his or her name. This was not merely a cultural idea. God Himself renamed people in the Old Testament to indicate a change in their identity. For example, He changed Abram's name, which meant "high father," to Abraham, which meant "father of many." He also changed Jacob's name, which meant "heel-grabber," "supplanter," or "deceiver," to Israel, indicating he had prevailed and had power with men and with God. Even in the New Testament, Jesus renamed Simon, which meant "to hear," as Peter, which meant "rock."

When Isaiah prophesied of a Son whose name would be Wonderful Counselor, this meant that the Son would be a wonderful, or miraculous, counselor. Likewise, the fact His name would be called Mighty God means that this Son would, indeed, be the Mighty God. Further, He would be the Everlasting Father and the Prince of Peace.

These are not mere labels; these words identify the Son. Obviously, this Son would not be a mere human. But on the other hand, the fact that this Son would rule upon the throne of David indicates He would also be a human descendant of David. How could it be that He would be human, but not merely human? The answer to this question is found in Gabriel's message to Mary. Her Son would be human, because He would be conceived by Mary in her womb. But He would not be merely human, for He would have no human father. Instead, Gabriel said, "The Holy Spirit will come upon you, and the power of the Highest will overshadow you; therefore, also, the Holy One who is to be born will be called the Son of God" (Luke 1:35).

Skeptics may deny the possibility of a conception in which both the human and divine are involved, but that is due to the rejection of the possibility of miracles. Mary did not understand how this could be, but Gabriel said, "With God nothing will be impossible" (Luke 1:37). This satisfied Mary, who did not reject the possibility of miracles. She answered, "Behold the maidservant of the Lord! Let it be to me according to your word" (Luke 1:38).

We should also consider the significance of the name Jesus. This name is formed from two Hebrew words. The first is Yah, which is an abbreviation for Yahweh, the covenant name by which God revealed Himself to Moses. Yahweh is the third person singular form of the Hebrew verb *hayah*. When God spoke to Moses from the burning bush, He identified Himself as *eheyeh*, which means I AM. This is the first person singular form of the same verb. Yahweh means "he is." The abbreviation "Yah" has the same meaning. So when God spoke of Himself to the Hebrew people, He identified Himself with the first person singular form of the verb *hayah*. When the people of Israel spoke of Him, they identified Him with the third person singular form of the same verb. The name Jesus is formed from this verb and from the Hebrew word *yasha*, which means "to deliver" or "to save." Thus, the name Jesus means "Yahweh-Savior" or "Yahweh will save." As the angel explained to Joseph, Mary's Son was to be called JESUS "for He will save His people from their sins" (Matthew 1:21). Since the Messiah's name identifies Him as Yahweh, the Savior, we can see how He can be identified by Isaiah not only as the Wonderful Counselor and the Prince of Peace, but also as the Mighty God and the Everlasting Father.

As Isaiah prophesied, the Messiah is the Branch of the LORD who will one day bring peace to the entire earth. Isaiah saw a vision of Him sitting on heaven's throne, wearing such an immense robe that its train filled Solomon's temple. He was identified by the seraphim as Yahweh. At the same time, He would be born of a virgin and would be God with us. It would be His birth of a virgin from David's lineage that would qualify Him to sit on David's throne, fulfilling the ancient prophecy of Nathan. But this descendant of David would also be the Mighty God, the Everlasting Father Himself.

With God, nothing shall be impossible!

9

More Prophecies from Isaiah

In his prison cell John the Baptist heard a report about the activities of Jesus. He sent two of his disciples to ask Jesus, "Are You the Coming One, or do we look for another?" (Matthew 11:3). Basing His answer on the prophecies of Isaiah, Jesus said, "Go and tell John the things which you hear and see: The blind see and the lame walk; the lepers are cleansed and the deaf hear; the dead are raised up and the poor have the gospel preached to them. And blessed is he who is not offended because of Me" (Matthew 11:4-6). Jesus' answer to John's question includes direct quotes from Isaiah as well as allusions to various prophecies made by Isaiah.

Isaiah 35 and More

First, note how closely Jesus' answer follows the prophecy found in Isaiah 35:5-6a: "Then the eyes of the blind shall be opened, and the ears of the deaf shall be unstopped. Then the lame shall leap like a deer, and the tongue of the dumb sing." Isaiah said, "The eyes of the blind shall be opened." Jesus said, "The blind see." Isaiah said, "The ears of the deaf shall be unstopped." Jesus said, "The deaf hear." Isaiah said, "The lame shall leap like a deer." Jesus said, "The lame walk."

John the Baptist had asked if Jesus were the Coming One. By quoting from Isaiah's prophecy about the Coming One, it is quite clear Jesus meant for John to understand the prophecies were indeed about Him. Not only did Jesus refer directly to Isaiah 35; He also alluded to other prophecies of Isaiah. For example, in one of Isaiah's messianic prophecies, a prophecy that Jesus specifically claimed to be fulfilled by His anointing with the Holy Spirit, Isaiah said, "The Spirit of the Lord GOD is upon Me, because the LORD has anointed me to preach good tidings to the poor" (Isaiah 61:1).[46] In His answer to John the Baptist, Jesus said, "The poor have the gospel preached to them."[47] Another possible connection between Jesus' words and Isaiah's prophecies is seen in Isaiah's statement, "Your dead shall live" (Isaiah 26:19). Jesus said, "The dead are raised up."

The last words of Jesus to the disciples of John the Baptist were, "And blessed is he who is not offended because of Me" (Matthew 11:6). These words echo Isaiah's prophecy that the LORD of hosts would be "a stone of stumbling and a rock of offense" (Isaiah 8:14). Earlier in his ministry, John the Baptist was certain Jesus was the Lamb of God who had come to take away the sin of the world.[48] Now that he was in prison, it was important for him to keep the faith. He must not stumble because of the adverse circumstances of life.

God Comes; He is Jesus

Now that we have looked at the specific texts in Isaiah from which Jesus formed His answer to John the Baptist, it will be helpful to go back and look at the larger contexts of those prophecies. First, the heart of Jesus' answer comes from Isaiah 35:5-6a: "Then the eyes of the blind shall be opened, and the ears of the deaf shall be unstopped. Then the lame shall leap like a deer, and the tongue of the dumb sing." Jesus referred to this text to indicate He was indeed the Coming One. These were the events happening in His ministry. Jesus healed the blind, the deaf, the lame, and those who could not speak. But Isaiah had said these events would happen at a specific point in time. That time is identified in the previous verse, Isaiah 35:4-6a: "Say to those who are fearful-hearted, 'Be strong, do not fear! Behold, your God will come with vengeance, with the recompense of God; He will come and save you.' Then the eyes of the blind shall be opened, and the ears of the deaf shall be unstopped. Then the lame shall leap like a deer, and the tongue of the dumb sing." Isaiah declared these miracles would occur when God came to save His people. Jesus fulfilled this prophecy, according to His own testimony to the disciples of John the Baptist. Thus, Jesus is God. If we examine the context of this prophecy even further, we discover the God in view here is none other than the LORD, Yahweh. Isaiah introduced this prophecy by saying, in part, "They shall see the glory of the LORD, the excellency of our God" (Isaiah 35:2b). This messianic prophecy, claimed by Jesus as His own, identifies Jesus as both LORD and God.

If, as seems quite likely, Jesus had Isaiah 8:14

in mind when He said, "And blessed is he who is not offended because of Me" (Matthew 11:6), this is a further identification of Jesus as Yahweh, the LORD of hosts. Isaiah said, "The LORD of hosts, Him you shall hallow; let Him be your fear, and let Him be your dread. He will be as a sanctuary, but as a stone of stumbling and a rock of offense" (Isaiah 8:13-14a). Rather than being offended because of Jesus, John the Baptist should have rejoiced to hear how Jesus was fulfilling the messianic prophecies of ancient Scripture.

A Prophecy of the Atonement

One of the most remarkable prophecies of the Messiah and His work begins in Isaiah 52:13 and continues through Isaiah 53. This extended prophecy explains in detail how the Messiah would suffer and die as our Sin-bearer, but it also anticipates His resurrection from the dead. We know this is a messianic prophecy because of the use made of it in the New Testament. First, in the evening after Jesus healed Peter's mother-in-law of her fever, many sick and demon-possessed people were brought to Jesus. With a word, Jesus cast out the spirits and healed all the sick.[49] Many of the evil spirits came out saying, "You are the Christ, the Son of God!" (Luke 4:41). It was not yet time for Jesus to be publicly proclaimed the Messiah, so He rebuked the spirits and did not allow them to say they knew that He was the Messiah.[50] In Matthew's account of this event, the healing and deliverance ministry of Jesus fulfilled that "which was spoken by Isaiah the prophet, saying: 'He Himself took our infirmities and bore our sicknesses'" (Matthew 8:17). This is a reference to Isaiah 53:4. Although many English translations render Isaiah 53:4 something like "He has borne our griefs and carried our sorrows," the literal meaning of the Hebrew word *chaliy*, translated "griefs," is sicknesses. The word translated "sorrows," *ka'av*, includes the meaning "pain." Matthew's connection of Jesus' ministry with Isaiah 53 is clear evidence, but not the only evidence, that the prophecy of Isaiah foretold the person and work of Jesus Christ. Another piece of evidence is found in Mark's account of the crucifixion of Jesus. Mark wrote, "With Him they also crucified two robbers, one on His right and the other on His left. So the Scripture was fulfilled which says, 'And He was numbered with the transgressors'" (Mark 15:27-28). This is a direct quote from Isaiah 53:12 which reads, in part, "He poured out His soul unto death, and He was numbered with the transgressors, and He bore the sin of many, and made intercession for the transgressors." But there is still a third bit of powerful evidence that Isaiah 53 is a prophecy of the Messiah. This evidence is found in the words of Jesus Christ Himself at the Last Supper just before His prayer in the Garden of Gethsemane. Jesus said to His disciples, "I say to you that this which is written must still be accomplished in Me: 'And He was numbered with the transgressors.' For the things concerning Me have an end" (Luke 22:37). Here Jesus, like Mark, quoted directly from Isaiah 53:12, asserting that Isaiah's prophecy was about Him. In the words of one translation, Jesus said, "For the time has come for this prophecy about me to be fulfilled: 'He was counted among those who were rebels.' Yes, everything written about me by the prophets will come true."[51]

In view of the evidence that Isaiah's prophecy was

about Jesus Christ, let's take a closer look at the content of that prophecy, which actually begins with Isaiah 52:13, identifying the Messiah as the LORD's Servant. After an opening focus on the Messiah's exaltation, the prophecy quickly turns to the marring of His appearance. Capturing in brief detail the full scope of His suffering, Isaiah said the Messiah's appearance "was marred more than any man, and His form more than the sons of men" (Isaiah 52:14). Although many people have suffered intensely, no one has ever suffered as much as the Messiah. We may have difficulty with this idea, because our view of Christ's sufferings and death, however realistic we wish to make it, always sanitizes the cross to some extent. We simply cannot comprehend the full impact of His wounds, bruises, and stripes. The marring of the Messiah was due not only to the physical consequences of being beaten to within an inch of His life, then crowned with thorns, then nailed brutally to a cross, and then being deeply pierced with the point of a spear, but also to the fact that in the midst of all this tortuous pain, He was also suffering the consequences of all the sins that ever had been or ever would be committed by the human race. The consequences of sin are both spiritual and physical, and for the sin of the entire world to be placed upon one completely innocent person in one experiential moment of time was indescribably devastating. It is no wonder that Jesus cried out, "My God! My God! Why hast thou forsaken me?"

Isaiah reiterated this idea early in his prophecy. He said, "He has no form or comeliness; and when we see Him, there is no beauty that we should desire Him" (Isaiah 53:2). Christ would be so disfigured that Isaiah said, "We hid, as it were, our faces from Him; He was despised, and we did not esteem Him" (Isaiah 53:3).

Laced throughout Isaiah's prophecy is the idea that the sufferings of the Messiah would be due to the fact that He would take upon Himself the sins of the human race: "He was wounded for our transgressions, He was bruised for our iniquities; the chastisement for our peace was upon Him, and by His stripes we are healed. All we like sheep have gone astray; we have turned, every one, to his own way; and the LORD has laid on Him the iniquity of us all" (Isaiah 53:5-6). As a lamb led to the slaughter and as a sheep before its shearers, Jesus did not open His mouth against those who oppressed and afflicted Him to protest His treatment.[52]

Isaiah foretold even the fact that the Messiah would be buried with the rich.[53] That this is indeed what happened can be seen in Matthew's account: "Now when evening had come, there came a rich man from Arimathea, named Joseph, who himself had also become a disciple of Jesus. This man went to Pilate and asked for the body of Jesus. Then Pilate commanded the body to be given to him. When Joseph had taken the body, he wrapped it in a clean linen cloth, and laid it in his new tomb which he had hewn out of the rock; and he rolled a large stone against the door of the tomb, and departed" (Matthew 27:57-60).

But not only did Isaiah foretell the sufferings, death, and burial of the Messiah, he also anticipated His resurrection from the dead. Isaiah said of the Messiah, "He shall see His seed, He shall prolong His days, and the pleasure of the LORD shall prosper in His hand" (Isaiah 53:10). After enduring excruciating pain and death, the Messiah would rise again to live forevermore. He would see His seed, all those who would believe on Him to become the sons of God, and He would prosper in everything that gave God pleasure. After His death, burial, and resurrection, the sin problem would be behind Him once and for all, and the only thing that would be before Him would be the pleasure of the LORD.

The Messiah's Anointing

After Jesus successfully resisted the temptations of Satan following forty days and nights of fasting, He returned to Galilee in the power of the Spirit. He had been brought up in Nazareth, and He returned there. As He was accustomed to doing, Jesus went to the synagogue on the Sabbath day. On this day, He was asked to read from the Book of Isaiah. Jesus located Isaiah 61 and read these words: "The Spirit of the LORD is upon Me, because He has anointed Me to preach the gospel to the poor; He has sent Me to heal the brokenhearted, to proclaim liberty to the captives and recovery of sight to the blind, to set at liberty those who are oppressed; to proclaim the acceptable year of the LORD" (Luke 4:18-19). This was a text that was quite familiar to the Jewish people in the first century. They no doubt had heard it read many times in that very synagogue. But something was different about this reading. When Jesus rolled up the scroll and gave it back to the synagogue attendant, He sat down. As everyone looked at Him, Jesus said, "Today this Scripture is fulfilled in your hearing" (Luke 4:21). His listeners marveled at these words. They could not imagine how Jesus could claim that Isaiah's prophecy was fulfilled there in the synagogue on that day. They said, "Is this not Joseph's son?" (Luke

4:22). To them, it seemed very bold for Jesus to make this claim. Before the day was over, all those in the synagogue were filled with wrath. They thrust Jesus out of Nazareth and attempted to cast Him over a cliff to His death.[54] As in a number of other cases, Jesus had quoted a specific messianic prophecy and identified Himself as its subject. As C. S. Lewis pointed out in his book *Mere Christianity*, we must accept Jesus' claims as to His identity, or we must reject them.[55] We have no other choice. He was either who He claimed to be, or He was not. Once we have accepted Jesus' claims by faith, we begin to see that He was, indeed, the primary subject of the Law, the Prophets, and the Psalms.

Every Knee Shall Bow

Other messianic prophecies in Isaiah may not be so well known, but they are nevertheless powerful indicators of the deity of Christ or of the identity of the Messiah. For example, these words of Yahweh, the LORD, are recorded: "There is no other God besides Me, a just God and a Savior; there is none besides Me. Look to Me, and be saved, all you ends of the earth! For I am God, and there is no other. I have sworn by Myself; the word has gone out of My mouth in righteousness, and shall not return, that to Me every knee shall bow, every tongue shall take an oath" (Isaiah 45:21-24). The New Testament church saw these words of Yahweh as having to do with Jesus Christ. Paul wrote that as a consequence of the Incarnation and Christ's willingness to die the humiliating death of the cross, "God also has highly exalted Him and given Him the name which is above every name, that at the name of Jesus every knee should bow, of those in heaven, and of those on earth, and of those under the earth, and that every tongue should confess that Jesus Christ is Lord, to the glory of God the Father" (Philippians 2:9-11). Since the background of Paul's statement is Isaiah's prophecy about every knee bowing and every tongue acknowledging Yahweh, Paul meant that the day is coming when every person will confess that Jesus Christ Himself is Yahweh. In the Old Testament, the Hebrew *Yahweh* is represented by the word LORD. So given its connection with Isaiah 45, Paul's statement that Jesus Christ is Lord is a radical acknowledgement of the identity of Jesus Christ.

The Gentiles Come to His Light

Another apparent messianic prophecy is found in Isaiah 60. In part this prophecy reads, "Arise, shine; for your light has come! And the glory of the LORD is risen upon you. For behold, the darkness shall cover the earth, and deep darkness the people; but the LORD will arise over you, and His glory will be seen upon you. The Gentiles shall come to your light, and kings to the brightness of your rising. ...The wealth of the Gentiles shall come to you, the multitude of camels shall cover your land, the dromedaries of Midian and Ephah; all those from Sheba shall come; they shall bring gold and incense, and they shall proclaim the praises of the LORD" (Isaiah 60:1-3, 5d-6). Early in Christian history interpreters viewed this prophecy as a reference to the magi who came from the East to Jerusalem searching for the King of the Jews. They had seen His star in the East and had come to worship Him. When they arrived at the house where the young child Jesus was staying with His mother Mary, the wise men fell down and worshiped Him.

Then they opened their treasures, giving Him gifts of gold, frankincense, and myrrh.[56]

Could it be that the visit of the wise men could indeed be a fulfillment of Isaiah's prophecy? Isaiah said, "The Gentiles shall come to your light, and kings to the brightness of your rising" (Isaiah 60:3). The wise men were Gentiles. And, as tradition holds, it is very possible that they should be viewed as kings. In biblical days, those we might today call tribal chieftains were identified as kings. Second, Isaiah said, "The wealth of the Gentiles shall come to you" (Isaiah 60:5d). Further, he identified that wealth as gold and incense. The wise men gave to Jesus gifts of gold, frankincense, and myrrh. It may seem too much, however, to think that, as Isaiah said, the multitude of camels ridden by or serving as pack animals for these wise men covered the land.[57] But this objection may owe a great deal to the idea that there were only three wise men. Scripture says nothing about how many wise men came to worship Jesus; the idea that there were three comes from the fact that three gifts are mentioned. As ancient Christian interpreters thought, it may indeed be that Isaiah foretold not only the Messiah's virgin birth, His death, burial, resurrection, and Second Coming, but also the visit of the Eastern wise men who worshiped Jesus and proclaimed the praises of the LORD.

The Definition of the Gospel

After reading messianic prophecies like those found in Isaiah, we can better understand why the apostle Paul identified the gospel as he did in his first letter to the believers at Corinth. Paul wrote, "Moreover, brethren, I declare to you the gospel, which I preached to you, which

135

also you received and in which you stand, by which also you are saved, if you hold fast that word which I preached to you—unless you believed in vain. For I delivered to you first of all that which I also received: that Christ died for our sins according to the Scriptures, and that He was buried, and that He rose again the third day according to the Scriptures" (I Corinthians 15:1-4). In this brief statement, Paul twice appealed to the Hebrew Scriptures. As Paul indicated, the Hebrew Scriptures foretold the death of the Messiah for our sins. They also foretold His resurrection on the third day. This is why the gospel is good news. Because of Christ's death, burial, and resurrection, the sin problem has been solved. Those who are willing to believe and obey the gospel have the assurance of salvation.

When you put your faith in Jesus Christ, the Messiah foretold by the Hebrew prophets, and when you obey the gospel message, you are identified with Him in His death, burial, and resurrection. Then you have the assured hope that you will one day spend eternity in the presence of the same LORD that Isaiah saw high and lifted up, who was seated upon a throne and whose train filled the temple of God. Like the seraphim in Isaiah's vision, you can one day cry out, "Holy, holy, holy is the LORD of hosts; the whole earth is full of His glory!"[58]

10

This Is That Which Was Spoken by the Prophet Joel

On the birthday of the church on the Day of Pentecost, the apostle Peter quoted extensively from the prophet Joel to explain the supernatural events of that day. After hearing the believers speak in a variety of languages they had never learned, the amazed and perplexed onlookers asked, "Whatever could this mean?" (Acts 2:12). Some, mocking, said, "They are full of new wine" (Acts 2:13). Standing up with the rest of the apostles, Peter said, "Men of Judea and all who dwell in Jerusalem, let this be known to you, and heed my words. For these are not drunk, as you suppose, since it is only the third hour of the day. But this is what was spoken by the prophet Joel" (Acts 2:14-16). Then, Peter proceeded to quote Joel 2:28-32: "And it shall come to pass in the last days, says God, that I will pour out of My Spirit on all flesh; your sons and your daughters shall prophesy, your young men shall see visions, your old men shall dream dreams. And on My menservants and on My maidservants I will pour out My Spirit in those days; and they shall prophesy. I will show wonders in heaven above and signs in the earth beneath: blood and fire and vapor of smoke. The sun shall be turned into darkness, and the moon into blood, before the coming of the great and awesome day of the LORD. And it shall come to pass that whoever calls on the name of the LORD shall be saved" (Acts 2:17-21).

A careful examination of Peter's Pentecost sermon indicates that he had more of Joel in mind than just Joel 2:28-32. The Book of Joel was foundational to his sermon; it appears not only in direct quotations, but also in verbal links and allusions. In addition, an examination of Acts 1 indicates the writer of Acts intentionally connected the events leading up to Peter's sermon with Joel. For example Joel wrote, "For in Mount Zion and in Jerusalem there shall be deliverance" (Joel 2:32). Luke records that Jesus commanded His disciples "not to depart from Jerusalem, but to wait for the Promise of the Father" (Acts 1:4). Further, Jesus said, "You shall be witnesses to me in Jerusalem, and in all Judea and Samaria, and to the end of the earth" (Acts 1:8).

It is significant that it was essential to be in Jerusalem to receive the promise of the Father, the baptism with the Holy Spirit.[59] Joel identified Jerusalem as the geographical location of deliverance. Deliverance would not stop there, however. Through the efforts of the disciples, it would spread over the earth.

Here is another link between Joel and Acts. Joel wrote, "I will pour out My Spirit on all flesh" (Joel 2:28). Luke recorded that Jesus said to His disciples, "You shall be baptized with the Holy Spirit ... you shall receive power when the Holy Spirit has come upon you" (Acts 1:5, 8). The promise given by Joel is identical with the promise given by Jesus. It was the outpouring of the Spirit.

Further, Joel wrote, "Your sons and your daughters shall prophesy ... On My menservants and on My maidservants I will pour out My Spirit in those days" (Joel 2:28, 29). Luke records that when the disciples had entered Jerusalem, "they went up into the upper room ... with the women and Mary the mother of Jesus, and with His brothers" (Acts 1:13-14). Joel's prophecy was egalitarian. Luke is careful to record that the waiting believers included not only the male, but female disciples.

Here is the fourth link we can see between Joel and Acts. In the first two verses of his book, Joel wrote, "When I bring back the captives of Judah and Jerusalem, I will also gather all nations" (Joel 3:1-2). Luke records that on the day of Pentecost, "There were dwelling in Jerusalem Jews, devout men, from every nation under heaven" (Acts 2:5-11). Joel's promise occurred in conjunction with a gathering of Jewish exiles. It included "all nations." Luke reports that on the Day of Pentecost, Jews were present "from every nation."

It is at least possible a fifth link between Joel and Acts can be seen in the references to new wine. One of the indications of the judgment of Yahweh in Joel was the drying up of the new wine. Upon Judah's repentance, however, the new wine would be restored in abundance.[60] On Pentecost, mockers judged the newly Spirit-filled believers to be "full of new wine."[61] Although they spoke from their unbelief, Luke may have used their statement to indicate a connection between Joel and the Pentecost event. It is within the ability of Scripture to present unbelievers as speaking divinely ordained words.

A definite connection between Joel and Acts is found in Peter's quote from Joel 2:28-32. Peter did not terminate his quote after Joel's reference to the Spirit; Peter included the references to wonders in the heavens and signs in the earth. The fact that Peter immediately followed this quote from Joel with a declaration that Jesus was attested by God "by miracles, wonders, and signs" indicates he connected these events in the life of Jesus with Joel's prophecy. Rather than dividing Joel's prophecy between events fulfilled on the Day of Pentecost and events yet to occur at the end of the age, Peter offered the events of Pentecost and the life of Jesus as the fulfillment of Joel. As F. F. Bruce has pointed out, "It was little more than seven weeks since the people in Jerusalem had indeed seen the sun turned into darkness, during the early afternoon of the day of our Lord's crucifixion. And on the same afternoon the paschal full moon may well have appeared blood-red in the sky as a consequence of that preternatural gloom. These were to be understood as tokens of the advent of the day of the Lord, 'that great and notable day,' a day of judgment, to be sure, but more immediately the day of God's salvation to all who invoked His name."[62] A careful comparison of Joel 2:30-31; 3:14-16 with Matt 27:45-54 suggests the events surrounding the death of Jesus could very well be a major fulfillment of Joel's prophecy. Although nothing is said in Matt 27:45-54 about blood, fire, and vapor of smoke, it is recognized by many scholars that these can be references not only to natural disasters but also to warfare.[63] Jesus had warned that the age would be characterized by war.[64] It may be, however, that in Peter's mind and for his purposes on the Day of Pentecost the reference to fire can be connected with the tongues as of fire that rested upon the believers and the reference to blood could be connected in the minds of the disciples with the crucifixion of Jesus, who had asked them to drink from a cup representing his blood (Matthew 26:27-28). Another clue suggesting that Peter may have had the events of the crucifixion in mind is the messianic theme of Psalm 18. Paul invested Psalm 18 with messianic meaning.[65] Comparison of Psalm 18:7-11 with Matthew 27:45, 51 shows close verbal linkage. Both texts refer to the shaking of the earth, quaking of the foundations of the hills (rocks splitting), and darkness. In this context, Psalm 18:8 reads, "Smoke went up from His nostrils, and devouring fire from His mouth; coals were kindled by it." This is symbolic language and we might dismiss any connection with the crucifixion of Christ except for the fact that Paul specifically reads Psalm 18 as a messianic text.

A seventh possible connection between Joel and Acts can be seen in Peter's answer to the question, "What shall we do?" (Acts 2:37). Joel wrote, "Tell your children about it, let your children tell their children, and their children another generation. ... 'Now therefore,' says the LORD, 'turn to Me with all your heart, with fasting, with weeping, and with mourning.' So rend your heart, and not your garments; return to the LORD your God, for He is gracious and merciful, slow to anger, and of great kindness; and He relents from doing harm. ... And it shall come to pass that whoever calls on the name of the LORD shall be saved. For in Mount Zion and in Jerusalem there shall be deliverance, as the LORD has said, among the remnant whom the LORD calls" (Joel 1:3; 2:12-13, 32).

The Book of Acts records Peter's words, "Repent, and be baptized every one of you in the name of Jesus Christ for the remission of sins, and ye shall receive the gift of the Holy Ghost. For the promise is unto you, and to your children, and to all that are afar off, *even* as many as the Lord our God shall call." (Acts 2:38-39, KJV).

In Peter's answer to the question, "What shall we do," there are thematic links to Joel and direct quotes from the prophet. Peter's command to repent summarizes Joel's call to turn to God with all one's heart, with fasting, weeping, mourning, and the rending of the heart. Peter's promise of remission of sins captures Joel's promise that God is gracious, merciful, slow to anger, and that he relents from doing harm. Peter's command to be baptized in the name of Jesus Christ is his answer to Joel's promise that whoever calls on the name of the LORD will be saved. Peter's statement that the promise of the Spirit is not only to those present, but also to their children and to all who are afar off is at least verbally linked with Joel's multigenerational idea. And the final words of Peter's statement, "as many as the Lord our God will call," are virtually identical to the Septuagint translation of Joel 2:32, "among the remnant whom the LORD calls."

The structure of Joel indicates the purposeful literary design of the book. The presence of Joel's ideas and words in the first two chapters of the Book of Acts is notable.

Did Peter think that Joel, as a prophet, foresaw Pentecost? If we take Peter's statement, "But this is what was spoken by the prophet Joel," at face value, coming to the text without any preconceived notion that the prophecy of Joel could not yet be fulfilled, or that it could be only partially fulfilled, Peter's statement certainly indicates he believed Joel prophesied about the Pentecost event. There is nothing in Peter's treatment of Joel to indicate he intended only to use Joel as an illustration or an application; there is nothing to indicate Peter believed Joel's prophecy could be divided between the outpouring of the Spirit and the wonders and signs. For Peter to follow his quote from Joel by noting the miracles, wonders, and signs done by God through Jesus gives strong contextual force to the idea Peter wanted his hearers to understand that Joel's prophecy was fulfilled.

But there is another point that gives even more strength to the idea that Peter saw Joel as anticipating Pentecost. That is, Peter's quotes from Psalm 16:8-11 are designed to authenticate the resurrection of Christ as the subject of prophecy. Peter followed this quote with these words: "David ... being a prophet, and knowing that God had sworn with an oath to him that of the fruit of his body, according to the flesh, He would raise up the Christ to sit on his throne, he foreseeing this, spoke concerning the resurrection of the Christ" (Acts 2:29-31). To Peter, the prophet David foresaw the resurrection of Christ. David did not think he was prophesying about himself. When Peter's references to Joel in Acts 2:16 and David in Acts 2:30-31 are placed side by side, little difference in meaning can be discerned between them. The fact David spoke knowingly indicates Joel did the same. There is nothing to indicate David was more aware of the import of his prophecy than was Joel.

But how does Peter's use of Joel contribute to the idea that the prophets spoke of Jesus? First, when Peter said those who had repented should be baptized in the name of Jesus Christ, he was interpreting Joel's statement "whoever calls on the name of the LORD shall be saved." When Joel referred to the name of the LORD, he used the covenant name by which God had revealed Himself to Israel: Yahweh. The name "Jesus" means "Yahweh-Savior." Peter was not the only New Testament figure to understand Joel's statement as an anticipation of baptism. When Ananias was sent by the Lord to Paul, after Paul's dramatic encounter with Jesus on the road to Damascus, he said to Paul, "And now why are you waiting? Arise and be baptized, and wash away your sins, calling on the name of the Lord" (Acts 22:16). Ananias, as well as Peter, connected Joel's prophecy about calling on the name of the Lord with baptism in the name of the Lord.

Further, Peter's use of Joel's prophecy contributes to the idea that the prophets spoke of Jesus because Peter used Joel's prophecy to affirm that Jesus was the promised Messiah. Immediately after his quote from Joel, Peter said, "Men of Israel, hear these words: Jesus of Nazareth, a Man attested by God to you by miracles, wonders, and signs which God did through Him in your midst, as you yourselves also know—Him, being delivered by the determined purpose and foreknowledge of God, you have taken by lawless hands, have crucified, and put to death; whom God raised up, having loosed the pains of death, because it was not possible that He should be held by it" (Acts 2:22-24). It seems quite clear that Peter viewed the miracles, wonders, and signs worked by Jesus, as well as His crucifixion, death, and resurrection, as fulfilling Joel's prophecy. Besides the three-hour darkness on the day of Christ's crucifixion, His resurrection and ascension were certainly marvelous signs in the earth and wonders in heaven.

After quoting both from Joel and the Book of Psalms, Peter said, "This Jesus God has raised up, of which we are all witnesses. Therefore being exalted to the right hand of God, and having received from the Father the promise of the Holy Spirit, He poured out this which you now see and hear" (Acts 2:32-33). The idea that the Holy Spirit was poured out by Jesus further connects Peter's message with Joel's prophecy in a messianic way. Joel had quoted the LORD God of Israel as saying, "I will pour out My Spirit on all flesh; your sons and your daughters shall prophesy, your old men shall dream dreams, your young men shall see visions. And also on My menservants and on My maidservants I will pour out My Spirit in those days" (Joel 2:28-29). But in Peter's message we discover the one who poured out the Holy Spirit was actually Jesus Himself. Since Jesus poured out the Spirit, He was the one to whom Joel referred when he said, "I will pour out My Spirit."

If Jesus received the promise of the Holy Spirit from the Father, how could He be identified as the LORD, Yahweh, by Joel? How could He be, as Peter asserts in Acts 2:36, both Lord and Christ, that is, both Yahweh—in Hebrew terms—and Messiah? The answer to these questions is bound up in the miracle of the Incarnation. In order for Jesus to be the Messiah, it was necessary for Him to be human. By definition, the Messiah is anointed by God. As Jesus said while reading from Isaiah 61 in the synagogue at Nazareth, "The Spirit of the LORD is upon Me, because He has anointed Me" (Luke 4:18a).

Jesus was fully and truly human. To deny this is to identify with antichrist, according to the apostle John, who wrote, "By this you know the Spirit of God: Every spirit that confesses that Jesus Christ has come in the flesh is of God, and every spirit that does not confess that Jesus Christ has come in the flesh is not of God. And this is the spirit of the Antichrist, which you have heard was coming, and is now already in the world" (I John 4:2-3). But at the same time Jesus was fully and truly God. As Paul wrote, "And without controversy great is the mystery of godliness: God was manifested in the flesh, justified in the Spirit, seen by angels, preached among the Gentiles, believed on in the world, received up in glory" (I Timothy 3:16). As John wrote in his gospel, "In the beginning was the Word, and the Word was with God, and the Word was God. ... And the Word became flesh and dwelt among us, and we beheld His glory, the glory as of the only begotten of the Father, full of grace and truth" (John 1:1, 14). To deny the deity of Christ is to declare He was a mere man, a claim that flies in the face of a multitude of Scriptures found in both the Old and New Testaments.

Does it seem too much to think that Jesus could be both God and man? This is where faith comes into focus. Faith is not about figuring out how miracles, like the Incarnation, could occur. Faith is about trusting God to be God and believing what His word declares to be true, even if we cannot reproduce His miracles in a science laboratory.

According to Scripture Jesus is both Lord and Christ. Because He was the Christ, the Messiah, Jesus received from the Father the promise of the Holy Spirit; because He was the Lord, He poured out His Spirit on the waiting believers on the Day of Pentecost. It was the amazing news that Jesus, whom they had crucified, was both Lord and Christ, that caused those who heard Peter to be cut to the heart and to ask Peter and the rest of the apostles, "Men and brethren, what shall we do?" (Acts 2:37). They would not have asked this question had they thought Jesus was merely a human being. It was the startling realization that He was both human and divine that provoked their response.

The Book of Joel refers to the Day of the LORD several times. The LORD of that day is none other than Jesus. He is the One who pours out His Spirit upon all flesh. He is the One who shows wonders in the heavens and in the earth. He is the One upon whose name we call for salvation. The proper response to this news is the same as it was on the Day of Pentecost. It is to repent and to be baptized in the name of Jesus Christ for the remission of sins and to receive His gift of the Holy Spirit.

PART III

How the Psalms Reveal Jesus

11

The Use of Psalms in
the New Testament

During His last meeting with His followers, Jesus said, "These are the words which I spoke to you while I was still with you, that all things must be fulfilled which were written in the Law of Moses and the Prophets and the Psalms concerning Me" (Luke 24:44). It is traditional to view the Hebrew Scriptures in these three categories. By referring to the Scriptures in this way, Jesus endorsed the entirety of the written Scriptures as they existed at that time.

Jesus' statement was extremely significant, in that it identified Him as the central theme of written revelation. In His account of Jesus' last moments on earth, Luke followed these words from Jesus by writing, "And He opened their understanding, that they might comprehend the Scriptures" (Luke 24:45). The idea here is that it is possible to understand the Old Testament only to the extent that one sees the Messiah as its central idea.[66] The significance of Jesus' statement is further seen in its connection to the Great Commission: "Thus it is written, and thus it was necessary for the Christ to suffer and to rise from the dead the third day, and that repentance and remission of sins should be preached in His name to all nations, beginning at Jerusalem" (Luke 24:46-47). The phrase "thus it is written" refers back to Christ's previous words about the theme of messianic prophecy running through the entire Old Testament. We may be sure the Hebrew Scriptures inform us of the sufferings of the Messiah and His resurrection from the dead, that the only proper response to the gospel of Jesus Christ is repentance, that the result of obedient faith is remission of sins, that the preaching of the gospel would originate in the Jewish community at Jerusalem, and that it would extend beyond that to all the Gentile nations of the world.

Unfortunately we do not know everything Jesus said to His followers when "He opened their understanding, that they might comprehend the Scriptures" (Luke 24:45). It is certain that at least some of what He said found its way into the preaching, teaching, and writing of the New Testament community. The church existed for something like fifteen years without any New Testament Scriptures. During this time the only scriptural authority was what we know today as the Old Testament. We can learn a great deal about the messianic theme of the Old Testament from the New Testament documents, but there is no indication that their exploration of the messianic theme is exhaustive. It may very well be that there were elements of messianic preaching and teaching that never found their way into the New Testament, even though they may have been well known among first-century believers. This is one reason it is profitable to study the Old Testament carefully with an awareness of its mes-

sianic theme; untold depths of christological riches wait
to be mined there.

Even though the writers of the New Testament may
not have been exhaustive in their treatment of the messianic content of the Old Testament, their exploration of
this central theme is rich and revealing. Let's look specifically at how selected New Testament texts reveal Christ
to be the theme of the Psalms.

Jesus and the Psalms

In an exchange with the Pharisees, Jesus asked,
"What do you think about the Christ? Whose Son is He?"
(Matthew 22:42a). They answered, "The Son of David"
(Matthew 22:42b). Jesus responded, "How then does
David in the Spirit call Him *'Lord,'* saying: *'The LORD
said to my Lord, sit at My right hand, till I make Your
enemies Your footstool'?* If David then calls Him *'Lord,'*
how is He his Son?" (Matthew 22:43-45). The Pharisees
were unable to answer, and this terminated their questions.[67] Jesus' appeal here to Psalm 110:1 as a messianic
text is quite significant. First, it reveals the Jewish scholars of the first century understood the messianic theme
of the Hebrew Scriptures. One of David's descendants
would actually be the Messiah.[68] Second, Jesus' use of
Psalm 110:1 endorses David as the author of the Psalm,
as indicated in the first line of the Psalm in the Hebrew
text.[69] Third, Psalm 110:1 indicates that although the
Messiah is David's Son—a human being—He is also in
some way David's Lord, requiring the Messiah to be more
than a human being.

Peter and the Psalms

In quotes from two psalms, Peter indicated on the Day of Pentecost that these psalms were messianic. First, in reference to the resurrection of Jesus from the dead, Peter said, "For David says concerning Him: 'I foresaw the LORD always before my face, for He is at my right hand, that I may not be shaken. Therefore my heart rejoiced, and my tongue was glad; moreover my flesh also will rest in hope. For You will not leave my soul in Hades, nor will You allow Your Holy One to see corruption. You have made known to me the ways of life; you will make me full of joy in Your presence'" (Acts 2:25-28). In this quote from the Septuagint translation of Psalm 16:8-11, Peter identified the Messiah as the theme of Psalm 16. In Psalm 16 we do not merely have a general principle applied to the Messiah; Peter said, "David says concerning Him." What David said was specifically about the Messiah.

Further, David knew he was writing about the Messiah. It was not that David thought he was writing about someone else, or he was setting forth general principles the Holy Spirit intended—without David's knowledge—to apply to the Messiah. Peter put it this way: "Men and brethren, let me speak freely to you of the patriarch David, that he is both dead and buried, and his tomb is with us to this day. Therefore, being a prophet, and knowing that God had sworn with an oath to him that of the fruit of his body, according to the flesh, He would raise up Christ to sit on his throne, he, foreseeing this, spoke concerning the resurrection of the Christ, that His soul was not left in Hades, nor did His flesh see corruption" (Acts 2:29-31). David was a prophet. He knew the Messiah would physically descend from him, and the Messiah would sit on his throne (i.e., the Messiah would exercise the royal authority of the Davidic lineage). David foresaw the resurrection of the Messiah and prophesied the Messiah's words concerning His resurrection when he wrote, "For You will not leave my soul in Hades, nor will You allow Your Holy One to see corruption" (Acts 2:27).

Then, just as Jesus had done, Peter appealed to Psalm 110:1 as a messianic text: "For David did not ascend into the heavens, but he says himself: 'The LORD said to my Lord, "Sit at My right hand, till I make Your enemies Your footstool" '" (Acts 2:34-35). When Jesus referred to this text, it was to inquire as to the Pharisees' understanding of the significance of David calling the Messiah his Lord. But Peter's use of the text indicates its connection to the resurrection. In other words, Psalm 110:1 does not describe the situation as it was when David wrote, but as it would be in the future upon the resurrection and ascension of the Messiah, Jesus. This is why David referred to God as LORD (*Yahweh*) and the Messiah as Lord (*Adonai*). Elsewhere, the Messiah is identified as LORD.[70] By definition, the Messiah is God as He is manifested in genuine and full human existence.[71] The Messiah certainly is *Yahweh*, but when a distinction is to be made, as in Psalm 110:1, between *Yahweh* and *Adonai* (when *Adonai* refers to the Messiah), that distinction is due to the human persona *Yahweh* assumed in the Incarnation. The humanness of the Messiah was not swallowed up or obliterated by His divine nature. Therefore the Messiah and God (*Yahweh*) can have conversations, and the Messiah can pray to God. This recognizes a distinction introduced by the Incarnation, but it does not radically separate God and the Messiah into two "persons," as we think of the word "person." The Messiah is just as much *Yahweh* as God is, but the Messiah is *Yahweh* in human existence. It may seem strange to think of *Yahweh* communicating with *Yahweh*, but if this were not possible the humanness of Jesus would be less than real, or the Incarnation would mean all there is to God is now limited to a human existence and God does not exist outside of Jesus.

For David to refer to the Messiah as *Adonai* does not suggest inferiority to *Yahweh*; it recognizes the humanness of the Messiah and the superiority of the Messiah to David, even though the Messiah is human. The theological purpose of Psalm 110:1 is not to inform us about the relationship between persons in the Godhead, but to inform us that David's human descendant is in some way his Lord, who—although He shares in humanity to such an extent that He can be addressed by *Yahweh*—is exalted to the place of greatest dignity and majesty in anticipation of the subjugation of the entire created realm to Him.[72] In Psalm 110:4 further evidence of the Messiah's humanity is seen in His identification by *Yahweh* as "a priest forever according to the order of Melchizedek." In order for the Messiah to be a priest, He had to stand in solidarity with those He represented to God. He had to be a human being representing other human beings to God.

It was not only on the Day of Pentecost that Peter appealed to the messianic theme of the Psalms as justification for preaching Jesus as the Messiah. Following the healing of the lame man at Gate Beautiful, Peter explained his actions to the Sanhedrin with these words: "Rulers of the people and elders of Israel: If we this day are judged for a good deed done to a helpless man, by what means he has been made well, let it be known to you all, and to all the people of Israel, that by the name of Jesus Christ of Nazareth, whom you crucified, whom God raised from the dead, by Him this man stands here before you whole. This is the 'stone which was rejected by you builders, which has become the chief cornerstone.' Nor is there salvation in any other, for there is no other name under heaven given among men by which we must be saved" (Acts 4:8-12).

The phrase "stone which was rejected by you builders, which has become the chief cornerstone" is a reference to Psalm 118:22. The author of Psalm 118 is not identified in the Old Testament or by Peter. The messianic theme is evident not only in verse 22,[73] but also in verses 25 and 26, which were quoted by the people who greeted Jesus as He rode into Jerusalem on a donkey.[74] To identify Jesus, the Messiah, as the chief cornerstone was quite significant in the Jewish milieu of the first century. The chief cornerstone was placed on the summit of the Temple in Jerusalem. To reject Jesus was to reject the final outworking of God's plan of redemption.[75]

To use these verses from Psalm 118 to refer to the Messiah is not the mere application of general principles. These verses have to do specifically with the Messiah, and it would be inappropriate to use them in reference to others. The messianic content of these verses was divinely intended to point to Jesus Christ.

The First-century Church and the Psalms

After their release by the Sanhedrin, Peter and John shared with their companions what the chief priests and elders had said. In response the community of believers prayed, "Lord, You are God, who made heaven and earth and the sea, and all that is in them, who by the mouth of Your servant David have said, 'Why did the nations rage, and the people plot vain things? The kings of the earth took their stand, and the rulers were gathered together against the LORD and against His Christ.' For truly against Your holy Servant Jesus, whom You anointed, both Herod and Pontius Pilate, with the Gentiles and the people of Israel, were gathered together ..." (Acts 4:24-27).

It is evident from their use of Psalm 2:1-2 in their prayer that the earliest believers viewed the psalm as a specific prophecy concerning the Messiah. Although the Hebrew text does not identify the author, the early church community assigned the psalm to David. It is possible the words of Psalm 2, identified as a Royal Psalm, were used upon the ascension of David's descendants to his throne. However, this is not the reason they are found in the inspired Scripture. Psalm 2 is included in the text specifically as a messianic psalm, a song about the coming Messiah, Jesus. The use of the psalm by the first believers identifies Jesus as the Anointed One of *Yahweh*, Herod and Pilate as included in the "kings of the earth" and "rulers" who rebelled against *Yahweh* and His Messiah, and "the Gentiles and the people of Israel" as included in "the nations [that] rage" and "the people [who] plot vain things."

Paul and the Psalms

Even though the content of Paul's preaching was not influenced by any human teacher—it was revealed directly to him by Jesus Christ—his use of the messianic theme of Psalms is virtually identical to Peter's use.[76]

Of course this is not surprising; the Holy Spirit inspired both men.

On his first missionary journey Paul's preaching at a synagogue in Antioch was deeply influenced by David's role as the Messiah's physical ancestor and by the prophetic implications of the Psalms. "He raised up for them David as king, to whom also he gave testimony and said, 'I have found David the son of Jesse, a man after My own heart, who will do all My will.' From this man's seed, according to the promise, God raised up for Israel a Savior—Jesus" (Acts 13:22-23).[77]

According to Paul, the Jewish community at Jerusalem and its religious leaders had condemned Jesus "because they did not know Him, nor even the voices of the Prophets which are read every Sabbath" (Acts 13:27). There was a connection between not knowing Jesus and not understanding the messianic content of the Prophets. In their ignorance the unbelieving Jews had fulfilled the Scriptures even while rejecting their message.[78]

The resurrection of Jesus was the fulfillment of "that promise which was made to the fathers" (Acts 13:32). As evidence that God had promised the fathers the Messiah would be resurrected, Paul offered these words from Psalm 2:7: "You are My Son, today I have begotten You" (Acts 13:33). Here Paul is in harmony with the believing Jewish community in Jerusalem in seeing Psalm 2 as a specific messianic prophecy.

As further evidence of the prophetic declaration of the resurrection of the Messiah in the Psalms, Paul quoted Psalm 16:10: "Therefore He also says in another Psalm: 'You will not allow Your Holy One to see corruption'" (Acts 13:35). These words had already been used by Peter to

159

point out that the psalms foretold the resurrection of the Messiah. Like Peter, Paul was careful to point out that David was not talking about himself, for he was still in his tomb and had seen corruption.[79] In his letter to the believers at Rome, Paul appealed to Psalm 69:9 as a messianic text: "For even Christ did not please Himself; but as it is written, 'The reproaches of those who reproached You fell on Me'" (Romans 15:3). This indicates that Paul saw this psalm of lament as having to do specifically with the Messiah.

Later in Romans 15, Paul pointed out that Psalm 18:49 indicates that the Jewish Messiah would also be the Messiah for the Gentiles: "Now I say that Jesus Christ has become a servant to the circumcision for the truth of God, to confirm the promises made to the fathers, and that the Gentiles might glorify God for His mercy, as it is written: 'For this reason I will confess to You among the Gentiles, and sing to Your name" (Romans 15:8-9).

Paul saw the messianic implications even of Psalm 117, using it in a contextual reference to Jesus Christ: "And again: 'Praise the LORD, all you Gentiles! Laud Him, all you peoples!" (Romans 15:11).[80] In a discussion of the events that would occur after the second coming of Christ, Paul wrote, "For 'He has put all things under His feet.' But when He says 'all things are put under Him,' it is evident that He who put all things under Him is excepted" (I Corinthians 15:27). Paul, like the writer of Hebrews,[81] saw Psalm 8 as a messianic psalm. It was not just a generic psalm about human beings that seemed to fit certain events in the life of Jesus. Under inspiration, it was placed in the Psalter for the specific purpose of indicating the Messiah would be a human being, made a little lower than the angels, but crowned with glory and honor and given dominion over the entire created realm. Paul saw the sub-jugation of all things under the Messiah as evidence of His resurrection.[82] If He did not rise from the dead, Psalm 8 would never be fulfilled.

Paul interpreted Psalm 68:18 as having to do spe-cifically with the Messiah: "But to each one of us grace was given according to the measure of Christ's gift. Therefore He says: 'When He ascended on high, He led captivity captive, and gave gifts to men.' (Now this, 'He ascended'—what does it mean but that He also first descended into the lower parts of the earth? He who descended is also the One who ascended far above all the heavens, that He might fill all things.)" (Ephesians 4:7-10). Psalm 68, then, foretells the ascension of the Messiah following His resurrection.

The Book of Hebrews and the Psalms

It is significant that the Book of Hebrews, written to Jewish believers in danger of defecting from their new-covenant faith in Christ, appeals repeatedly to a variety of psalms to assert that Jesus, the true Messiah, is supe-rior to everything associated with the law of Moses. He is the fulfillment of all Jewish messianic hopes.

Since the law of Moses was given by angels,[83] it was important for the writer of Hebrews to show the superi-ority of Christ over the angels. This is an extended text that begins with a quote from Psalm 2:7: "For to which of the angels did He ever say: 'You are My Son, today I have begotten You'?" (Hebrews 1:5a). Psalm 2 is a mes-sianic psalm that begins with the question, "Why do the nations rage, and the people plot a vain thing? The kings of the earth set themselves, and the rulers take counsel together, against the LORD and against His Anointed, saying, 'Let us break Their bonds in pieces and cast away Their cords from us'" (Psalm 2:1-3). The Hebrew word translated "Anointed" is *Mashiyach*, from which comes the Greek *Messias* and the English "Messiah." First-century believers understood these verses to refer to the involvement of the unbelieving Romans and Jews, including Herod and Pilate, in crucifying Jesus.[84] The LORD's response to this rebellion is found in Psalm 2:4-6: "He who sits in the heavens shall laugh; the LORD shall hold them in derision. Then He shall speak to them in His wrath, and distress them in His deep displeasure: 'Yet I have set My King on My holy hill of Zion.'" The LORD is not the least perturbed by rebellion against the Messiah; nothing can thwart His divine purpose. Although Jesus was rejected and crucified by unbelieving Gentiles and Jews, that would not prevent Him from reigning as King on the holy hill of Zion. His resurrection would overcome the effects of their rebellion.

For the specific purposes of the Book of Hebrews, the next verse in Psalm 2 demonstrates that Jesus had an identity superior to that of angels. This identity is found in the prophetic words of the Messiah: "I will declare the decree: The LORD has said to Me, 'You are My Son, today I have begotten you'" (Psalm 2:7). Although angels are occasionally called the sons of God in the Old Testament, they were never the sons of God in the way that the Messiah was the Son of God; He was the Son of God by virtue of having been begotten of God. He was not a created being like the angels.

The superiority of Jesus over the angels is also seen in that, while the angels are spirit beings made by God,

the Son is God Himself. The Book of Hebrews estab-
lishes this by two quotes from the book of Psalms. First,
from Psalm 104:4, Hebrews reads, "And of the angels He
says: 'Who makes His angels spirits and His ministers a
flame of fire'" (Hebrews 1:7). Second, from Psalm 45:6-
7, Hebrews reads, "But to the Son He says: 'Your throne,
O God, is forever and ever; a scepter of righteousness is
the scepter of Your kingdom. You have loved righteousness and hated lawlessness; therefore God, Your God,
has anointed You with the oil of gladness more than Your
companions" (Hebrews 1:8-9). The Son is superior to the
angels because He is not merely a created spirit being;
He is God manifest in human existence; both aspects of
His identity are seen in this quote from Psalm 45:6-7. His
deity is seen in verse 6: He is God, whose throne is eternal. His humanity is seen in verse 7: as the Messiah, He is
anointed with the oil of gladness, the Holy Spirit.

In a quote from Psalm 102:25-27, the Book of
Hebrews identifies Jesus as Yahweh Himself. According
to the Book of Hebrews the following words from the
Book of Psalms are addressed to the Son: "You, LORD, in
the beginning laid the foundation of the earth, and the
heavens are the work of Your hands. They will perish,
but You remain; and they will all grow old like a garment; like a cloak You will fold them up, and they will
be changed. But You are the same, and Your years will
not fail" (Hebrews 1:10-12). Since Jesus is Yahweh, the
Creator, He is certainly superior to the angels, who are
created.[85]

Psalm 110:1, also used by Jesus[86] and Peter[87] as a reference to the Messiah, is seen in Hebrews 1:13 as further
evidence of the Messiah's superiority over the angels: "But

163

to which of the angels has He ever said: 'Sit at My right hand, till I make Your enemies Your footstool'?" This has never been said to any angel. Jesus is not an angel; He is the Messiah, and He has ascended to the place of ultimate honor, majesty, and power—symbolized by the idea of the right hand of God or, as the Book of Hebrews says, "the right hand of the Majesty on high" (Hebrews 1:3). As F. F. Bruce has pointed out, this is not a reference to a specific spatial location: "That no literal location is intended was as well understood by Christians in the apostolic age as it is by us: they knew that God has no physical right hand or material throne where the ascended Christ sits beside Him; to them the language denoted the exaltation and supremacy of Christ as it does to us."[88]

Further indicating the superiority of Christ over the angels, the writer of Hebrews joined Paul in viewing Psalm 8 as having to do with the incarnation and exaltation of the Messiah. Hebrews reads, "For He has not put the world to come, of which we speak, in subjection to angels. But one testified in a certain place, saying: 'What is man that You are mindful of him, or the son of man that You take care of him? You have made him a little lower than the angels; you have crowned him with glory and honor, and set him over the works of Your hands. You have put all things in subjection under his feet.' For in that He put all in subjection under him, He left nothing that is not put under him. But now we do not yet see all things put under him. But we see Jesus, who was made a little lower than the angels, for the suffering of death crowned with glory and honor, that He, by the grace of God, might taste death for everyone" (Hebrews 2:5-9).

Paul understood the same text from the Book of Psalms as a reference to Christ. He wrote, "For 'He has put all things under His feet.' But when He says 'all things are put under Him,' it is evident that He who put all things under Him is excepted" (I Corinthians 15:27).

This example given by the writer of Hebrews as to the superiority of the Son of God over angels concerns the Incarnation. Although the Son of God is God manifest in genuine, authentic, and complete humanity,[89] and although human beings are "a little lower than the angels" (Hebrews 2:7, 9), Jesus is nevertheless superior to the angels because He is "crowned with glory and honor" (Hebrews 2:9).

The Septuagint translation of Deuteronomy 32:8 indicates that God has put this present world in subjection to angels: "When the Most High divided the nations, when he separated the sons of Adam, he set the bounds of the nations according to the number of the angels of God." Since the Book of Hebrews frequently appeals to the Septuagint, it may be that this is the intended reference behind the declaration that God "has not put the world to come ... in subjection to angels." Angelic administration over specific nations of the world is further suggested by references to "the prince of Persia" and "the prince of Greece" (Daniel 10:13, 20). Michael is seen as "one of the chief princes" (Daniel 10:13) and as the prince of Israel (Daniel 10:21; 12:1). This reference, in conjunction with Deuteronomy 32:9, suggests that while God has given other angels some kind of administrative responsibility over the various nations of the world, He has given Michael this responsibility over Israel.

The superiority of the Son of God over the angels is seen in that the "world to come," or the ultimate and final age, will be under subjection to Him, not to angels.[90]

So the Book of Hebrew quotes Psalm 8:4-6 as a Messianic reference; although the Messiah is the Son of God, He is also the Son of Man—a genuine human being, and He is thus one who has been "made ... a little lower than the angels" and who has been "crowned ... with glory and honor." He will be set over the works of God's hands and have all things put in subjection under His feet. Although "we do not yet see all things put under him,"[91] it is clear that this is His ultimate destiny. As Paul pointed out, "Christ ... is over all, the eternally blessed God" (Romans 9:5). The superiority of the Son of God over the angels is seen in that, although in the Incarnation He assumed a status "a little lower" as a human being, He will rule over all creation, including the angels themselves.

The writer of Hebrews understood not only Psalm 110:1 to be about the Messiah, but also Psalm 110:4: "The LORD has sworn and will not relent, 'You are a priest forever according to the order of Melchizedek'." This verse is quoted four times in the Book of Hebrews. The fact the Messiah's high priesthood was from Melchizedek and not from Levi indicates the superiority of His priesthood over the priesthood associated with the law of Moses. This is because Melchizedek predated Levi and because Abraham, the great patriarch of the Hebrew people, paid tithe to Melchizedek.[92]

Psalm 22, claimed by Jesus as His own prayer when He prayed the words of the first verse on the cross, is identified in the Book of Hebrews as a psalm about the Messiah. The Book of Hebrews reads, "For both He who

166

sanctifies and those who are being sanctified are all of one, for which reason He is not ashamed to call them brethren, saying: 'I will declare Your name to My brethren; in the midst of the assembly I will sing praise to You'" (Hebrews 2:11-12). This quote is from Psalm 22:22, and it addresses the Messiah's humanity, not His deity. He declares His solidarity with the human race even to the point of lifting up His voice in praise to God "in the midst of the assembly," or in the midst of the church.

According to Hebrews 10:5-9, the Messiah's willingness to surrender to the will of God in providing Himself as the atonement for sin is seen in Psalm 40:6-8. The Book of Hebrews reads, "Therefore, when He came into the world, He said: 'Sacrifice and offering You did not desire, but a body You have prepared for Me. In burnt offerings and sacrifices for sin You had no pleasure. Then I said, "Behold, I have come—in the volume of the book it is written of Me—to do your will, O God." Previously saying, 'Sacrifice and offering, burnt offerings, and offerings for sin You did not desire, nor had pleasure in them' (which are offered according to the law), then He said, 'Behold, I have come to do Your will, O God.' He takes away the first that He may establish the second. By that will we have been sanctified through the offering of the body of Jesus Christ once for all" (Hebrews 10:5-10).

This passage from Psalm 40:6-8 is incarnational. It has to do with what the Messiah said to God in conjunction with His entrance into the world. The statement "a body You have prepared for Me" indicates the entire quote was made after the Incarnation when the Messiah was existing in the body so prepared.

The sacrifices, offerings, burnt offerings, and sacrifices for sin in view here are those "which are offered according to the law" (Hebrews 10:8). That is, the reference here is not to abuses of the sacrificial system of the law of Moses, but to the sacrificial system itself, as found in the Law. This indicates the temporary nature of the law.

God did not give Israel the law because it was His ultimate plan for redemption or even because there was something inherent in the sacrificial system that pleased Him. He gave Israel the law to demonstrate clearly to them the sinfulness of human nature, their inability to redeem themselves, and their desperate need for a Savior. This is what is meant by Paul's statement that "the law was our tutor to bring us to Christ, that we might be justified by faith" (Galatians 3:24).

The Messiah came to do the will of God, which in this context, was to take away the first covenant with its ineffectual sacrifices and to replace it with the New Covenant by means of "the offering of the body of Jesus Christ once for all" (Hebrews 10:9-10).

The phrase "in the volume of the book it is written of Me" indicates the Christ-centered nature of the Hebrew Scriptures. As Jesus said, everything that is written concerning Him in the Law of Moses, the Prophets, and the Psalms must be fulfilled.[93] Jesus also said to the unbelieving Jews, "You search the Scriptures, for in them you think you have eternal life; and these are they which testify of me" (John 5:39). The Pharisees thought eternal life was to be found in the study of the Scriptures alone; they did not understand the very Scriptures they studied spoke of Jesus. To the disciples on the road to Emmaus, Jesus began "at Moses and all the Prophets" and "expounded to them in all the Scriptures the things concerning Himself" (Luke 24:27).

The appearance of a portion of Psalm 40:6-8 in Hebrews 10:9-10 underscores the relationship between the law of Moses and the New Covenant. Here the Book of Hebrews clarifies the fact that the sacrifices, offerings, burnt offerings and offerings for sin were those "which are offered according to the law." This means the problem with the sacrifices was not the attitude of those who offered them or the spiritual condition of Israel at large. In other words, the reason God did not desire these sacrifices or take pleasure in them was not because of lack of devotion or faith on the part of those offering the sacrifices. The sacrifices were offered according to the law, but they still brought Him no pleasure. They could not, for they were incapable of taking away sins under the best of conditions. God could not be satisfied with a mere shadow. In a dramatic statement which should answer forever the relationship of the Old Covenant to the New Covenant, Hebrews 10:9 declares, "He takes away the first that He may establish the second." The "first" is the Old Covenant with its inadequate sacrificial system; the "second" is the New Covenant with its efficacious offering. Herein it is clearly seen that the two covenants cannot coexist. The New Covenant is not merely an updated or revised or enhanced version of the Old Covenant. For the New Covenant to be in effect, the Old Covenant had to be taken away. There is no compatibility between these covenants. One is a shadow; the other is the reality.

In the inspired attempt to convince wavering Jewish believers to retain their faith in Christ, the writer of Hebrews could find no richer resource than the messianic psalms. These were the Scriptures the original readers of Hebrews believed without question, the words their ancestors had long clung to in hopes of deliverance: They were fulfilled in Jesus Christ.

The Book of Revelation and the Psalms

Another powerful indicator that we should read the Book of Psalms as a book about the Messiah is found in Revelation 2:26-27, where Jesus, the Son of God, claimed Psalm 2:7-9 as a reference to His authority. He said, "And he who overcomes, and keeps My works until the end, to him I will give power over the nations—'He shall rule them with a rod of iron; They shall be dashed to pieces like the potter's vessels'—as I also have received from My Father." He thus authenticated the view of the early believers,[94] Paul,[95] and the writer of Hebrews[96] that Psalm 2 is about the Messiah. Since Psalms 1-2 function together as an introduction to the Book of Psalms, establishing the essential themes of the entire book and providing an interpretive framework for everything that follows, this is quite significant. Jesus believed the psalms were about Him; His understanding of the psalms is authoritative for us.

But this is not the last use of the psalms in Revelation. In a dramatic description of the Second Coming, John wrote that he saw heaven opened. A white horse came forth, ridden by One who was called Faithful and True. This rider, whose eyes are like a flame of fire and upon whose head are many crowns, judges and makes war in righteousness. He has a name known to no one except Himself. His robe is dipped in blood, and His name is "The Word of God." Armies in heaven follow Him on white horses. They are clothed in fine linen, symbolizing the righteousness of the saints.[97] In a graphic description that reaches back to Psalm 2:8-9, John wrote, "Now out of His mouth goes a sharp sword, that with it He should strike the nations. And He Himself will rule them with a rod of iron" (Revelation 19:15). Some one thousand years before John had this vision, David had written these words that function as an introduction to the entire Book of Psalms: "Ask of Me, and I will give You the nations for Your inheritance, and the ends of the earth for your possession. You shall break them with a rod of iron; you shall dash them to pieces like a potter's vessel" (Psalm 2:8-9). These words anticipate the Second Coming of Christ. Their fulfillment, like all of the messianic prophecies found in the Hebrew Scriptures, is certain.

The declaration of Jesus that the Law of Moses, the Prophets, and the Psalms are about Him should motivate us to search for Him in the Hebrew Bible. That is what the New Testament believers did, and we are forever enriched by it. We grow in our knowledge of the Lord and Savior, Jesus Christ, as we discover what the Hebrew Scriptures say about Him.

12

David's View of the Psalms

In his last words, David wrote, "Thus says David the son of Jesse; thus says the man raised up on high, the anointed of the God of Jacob, and the sweet psalmist of Israel: The Spirit of the LORD spoke by me, and His word was on my tongue. The God of Israel said, the Rock of Israel spoke to me: 'He who rules over men must be just, ruling in the fear of God. And he shall be like the light of the morning when the sun rises, a morning without clouds, like the tender grass springing out of the earth, by clear shining after rain.' Although my house is not so with God, yet He has made with me an everlasting covenant, ordered in all things and secure, for this is all my salvation and all my desire; will He not make it increase? But the sons of rebellion shall all be as thorns thrust away, because they cannot be taken with hands. But the man who touches them must be armed with iron and the shaft of a spear, and they shall be utterly burned with fire in their place" (II Samuel 23:1-7).

When the Bible records the last words of someone, we should take special notice. Last words tend to be theologically significant, and that is certainly the case with these last words of David. They express the inspiration and content of his psalms and the certainty of the Davidic Covenant.

David Was Inspired

David asserted the inspiration of his words when he wrote, "The Spirit of the LORD spoke by me, and His word was on my tongue. The God of Israel said, the Rock of Israel spoke to me. ..." The inspiration of David's words is confirmed by Jesus: "For David himself said by the Holy Spirit ..." (Mark 12:36). Peter understood the psalms of David to be inspired: "Men and brethren, this Scripture had to be fulfilled, which the Holy Spirit spoke before by the mouth of David concerning Judas, who became a guide to those who arrested Jesus" (Acts 1:16). The first-century church understood the words of David to be the words of God: "So when they heard that, they raised their voice to God with one accord and said: 'Lord, You are God, who made heaven and the earth and the sea, and all that is in them, who by the mouth of Your servant David have said ...'" (Acts 4:24-25). No distinction is made between the Lord God and the Holy Spirit as the actual Author of David's words.

David Wrote about the Messiah

The content of David's psalms is messianic, as may be seen in his words, "He who rules over men must be just, ruling in the fear of God. And he shall be like the light of the morning when the sun rises, a morning without clouds, like the tender grass springing out of the earth, by clear shining after rain" (II Samuel 23:3b-4). In this description of a just ruler, David was not talking about himself or any of his merely human descendants. He said, "Although my house is not so with God ..." (II Samuel 23:5).

In the psalms, the Messiah is frequently associated with banishing darkness by bringing light.[98] His rule is noted by justice.[99] Further evidence that David wrote intentionally and knowingly about the Messiah can be seen in an examination of the Hebrew text of II Samuel 23:1 and in a survey of the history of the interpretation of the text.

Young's Literal Translation (1862/1898) renders II Samuel 23:1: "And these are the last words of David:—'The affirmation of David son of Jesse—And the affirmation of the man raised up—Concerning the Anointed of the God of Jacob, And the Sweetness of the Songs of Israel.'" The word translated "on high" (*'al*) by the KJV and many modern English translations may also be translated "concerning." The difference in meaning between the two translations is that the translation "on high" makes David "the anointed of the God of Jacob," or the messianic person. The translation "concerning" makes the Messiah someone other than David and the subject of David's words. The phrase "anointed of the God of Jacob"[100] contains the word that finds its way by transliteration into the New Testament as a reference to Christ: *Meshiyach* becomes "Messias" or "Messiah." The meaning is the same as the Greek *Christos*. Both words mean "anointed."

That the translation should be "concerning" and not "on high" is indicated not only by the contextual reference to the Messiah in II Samuel 23:3-4, but also by the history of the interpretation of the text. With the finalization of the form of the Hebrew text by the Masoretic ("traditionalist") scribes in about AD 1000, there arose a series of Jewish commentators who determined the meaning of the Hebrew text for the Jewish communities. One of the most influential of these commentators was Rashi, who was born in about AD 1040. Rashi did not believe that the Messiah had come. During this time of the Crusades, European Jews were being forced to convert to Christianity. Rashi's mission was to give the Jewish people a biblical ground to resist conversion to Christianity. The way he chose to do this was to take passages that could be understood as references to the Messiah and to explain them in light of some historical figure. He identified messianic prophecies as being fulfilled by David or Solomon. Rashi did this by introducing glosses in the margins of the Hebrew text with these interpretations. Rashi's interpretation was called the Peshat, the Hebrew word that means "simple." According to Erwin Rosenthal, a leading Rashi scholar of the twentieth century, Rashi was willing to sacrifice messianic hope to resist Christian interpretation.[101]

The Septuagint, a Greek translation of the Hebrew Scriptures dating from about 250 BC, was much more messianic than the Masoretic text of AD 1000. The Septuagint sees II Samuel 23:1 as indicating that David wrote about the Messiah. The Septuagint was in common use in first-century Jewish communities and became the Bible of the first century Christian church. Because of the use of this Greek translation by the followers of Jesus, the non-messianic Jewish communities gradually turned from the Septuagint.

The reformers Martin Luther and John Calvin championed the turn from the Latin Vulgate to the Hebrew text. At that time, no Christian commentaries had been written on the Hebrew text, so Luther and Calvin went to Rashi's interpretations, viewing them as the "original historical" meaning. Rashi's interpretations were, however, non-messianic.

The influence of the reformers on current Christian interpretation can be seen in the view that the messianic texts are first about some historic person or persons in ancient Israel and only by application, reinterpretation, or fuller meaning about the Messiah.[102]

II Samuel 23 indicates the certainty of the Davidic Covenant in spite of the unfaithfulness of David's descendants in the statement, "Although my house is not so with God, yet He has made with me an everlasting covenant, ordered in all things and secure" (II Samuel 23:5a). Ultimately, the Messiah will sit on David's throne, fulfilling the promise God made to David.[103] II Samuel 23 indicates that David was aware of the prophetic nature of the psalms. Their messianic content was not hidden from him. Although the events and persons he described were rooted in actual history, they were intended by him to represent the coming Messiah. When Peter declared David was a prophet who spoke knowingly about the Messiah and who foresaw messianic events, he intended his words to be taken literally.[104] Rather than the messianic content of the psalms being a result of reinterpretation by the first-century church or of "fuller meaning," it is the result of David's intention.

The Purpose of the Book of Psalms

What purpose does the Book of Psalms serve? The psalms have been widely used as devotional literature, giving comfort and hope to those who are in difficult circumstances. Many people have favorite psalms they love to quote or to meditate on, like Psalm 1, 8, 23, or 91. The beautiful words and well-timed cadences of the Psalter sooth troubled hearts. They assure us we are walking on a path others have trod before us, and if we trust in our Lord, there is the promise of a better day.

But there is something in the psalms that goes far beyond this. The Psalter is first and foremost a book about the Messiah. This does not mean only that there are a few "messianic" psalms scattered throughout the book. The entire Psalter, from beginning to end, testifies of the Messiah. When read as a messianic book, Psalms takes on a dynamic dimension beyond that of devotional literature. It is no longer a section of the Bible we turn to only when we are searching for encouragement or wisdom; it is a book we turn to order to know Jesus better. This does not eliminate its devotional value; it enhances it. Now we see the One with whom we identify in suffering and victory is not just David or other human authors; it is our Lord Jesus Christ.

As we seek to understand the Book of Psalms, we should note that it consists of psalms written by a wide variety of authors over a large span of time. The earliest psalm was written by Moses; the latest was written during the time of the Babylonian exile or perhaps even afterwards as the Israelites returned to their land. They were written over a span of some one thousand years. The individual psalms were inspired as originally written. In their

178

original form, they had to do with the person identified in the superscription,[105] but the Holy Spirit often intended that person to represent, in some way, the ultimate Son of David, the Messiah, or for the psalm to advance the messianic theme of the entire book. It is indicated by II Samuel 23:1-7 that David knew he was writing about the Messiah.[106] This was certainly Peter's view.[107] The final composition of the Psalter was also inspired, so that the arrangement of the psalms within the book gives us an inspired interpretation of the psalms.

The framework of the Psalter is messianic: It focuses on Zion theology and the kingdom of God, by which we mean the physical restoration of Davidic hope, the ultimate fulfillment of the promise God made to David that the Messiah would descend physically from him to rule on David's throne in Zion. By means of the psalms, those who read them can see how God intervened on behalf of people of faith in history, and they can be encouraged to trust God in the midst of their own adversities. The selection and arrangement of the psalms are intended to explore the relationship between the law of Moses and Israel's hope for the future, or, as we might say from the Christian perspective, the relationship between law and grace. The final form of the Psalter is also intended to explore the meaning of the Davidic Covenant in view of the apostasy and exile of the house of David.

The Introduction to the Book of Psalms

The placement of the first two psalms makes them an obvious introduction to the entire Psalter. The first psalm pronounces a blessing on "the man who walks not in the counsel of the ungodly, nor stands in the path of sinners, nor sits in the seat of the scornful" (Psalm 1:1), implying that walking in the counsel to be found in the Book of Psalms is the source of blessing.

Psalm 1 is known as a Torah, or law, psalm because it describes the blessed man as one who delights "in the law of the LORD" and who meditates "in His law ... day and night" (Psalm 1:2). The word *torah* means "instruction," and it is used with a variety of meanings. Here, it is apparently not a reference to the law of Moses, but to the psalms themselves. In other words, Psalm 1:2 does not mean that the reader would be better off meditating in the law of Moses than in the psalms! The psalms offer wise instruction and godly counsel.

Psalm 1, a Torah psalm, is connected conceptually with Psalm 2, a royal messianic psalm. This is a pattern in the Psalter. Psalm 19, another Torah psalm,[108] is connected with Psalms 20-21, royal messianic psalms.[109] Psalm 119, a Torah psalm,[110] is connected to the section of psalms known as Songs of Ascents,[111] with their royal messianic focus.[112] For the Torah psalms to be attached to royal messianic psalms in this way follows an ancient method of interpretation by attachment. In other words, to attach the messianic psalm to the Torah psalm serves to provide interpretation for the Torah psalm. The concept of law must be interpreted in connection with the concept of the Messiah.

Psalm 1 begins by pronouncing a blessing upon the person who delights in the law (*torah*, "instruction," a reference here to Scripture) of the LORD (Psalm 1:2); Psalm 2 ends by pronouncing a blessing on all who put their trust in the Son, the Messiah (Psalm 2:12b). The idea presented here is that meditation upon the Scripture leads to trust in the Messiah.[113] The word translated "trust" (*chasah*) is used in the Old Testament with the same essential meaning as the New Testament words "faith" and "believe." The word means "to take refuge." This helps us understand the New Testament word translated "faith," which is used essentially as a synonym for the Old Testament "trust."

Contrary to a view that arose during the twentieth century, biblical faith is not about some kind of mental perspective, manipulation, or gymnastics by which one cajoles God into fulfilling one's desires. Faith is not, in the strictest sense, a way of thinking. It is trust in God in the sense of taking refuge in Him in time of trouble and believing Him to be who He claims to be and to do what He promises to do.

The "counsel of the ungodly ... the path of sinners ... the seat of the scornful" (Psalm 1:1) is a series of terms further described in Psalm 2:1 as plotting "a vain thing." The "counsel of the ungodly" is seen in Psalm 2:2 as "the rulers take counsel together, against the LORD and against His Anointed [the Messiah]." It is ungodly counsel that leads kings and rulers to say, "Let us break Their bonds in pieces and cast away Their cords from us" (Psalm 2:3).

Psalm 1 declares of the ungodly that they are "like the chaff which the wind drives away. Therefore the ungodly shall not stand in the judgment, nor sinners in the congregation of the righteous. ... the way of the ungodly shall perish" (Psalm 1:4-6). According to Psalm 2, this happens because "He who sits in the heavens shall laugh; the LORD shall hold them in derision. Then He shall speak to them in His wrath, and distress them in His deep displeasure" (Psalm 2:4-5). The Messiah will "break them [the nations that follow ungodly counsel] with a rod of iron ... [and] dash them to pieces like a potter's vessel" (Psalm 2:9).[114] The Son will be angry with those who do not kiss Him—as an act of respect and homage—and they will "perish in the way, when His wrath is kindled but a little" (Psalm 2:12).

The person who rejects the ungodly counsel that encourages people to cast off loyalty to the LORD and His Messiah and who instead delights and meditates in the Scripture will, in contrast to the fate of those who rebel, "be like a tree planted by the rivers of water, that brings forth its fruit in its season, whose leaf also shall not wither" (Psalm 1:3). The wise man is like a healthy, fruitful, enduring tree. The man who follows ungodly counsel is like chaff. The wind will drive him away; he will perish.[115] The response of the LORD to those who follow ungodly counsel is to laugh and to hold them in derision (Psalm 2:4). In wrath He will speak to them and distress them. The distressing proclamation the LORD makes to those who seek to rebel is this: "Yet I have set My King on My holy hill of Zion" (Psalm 2:6). In their desire to cast off the authority of the LORD and His Messiah, the people are plotting "a vain thing" (Psalm 2:1). It is vain because God has set His King, the Messiah, on Zion. The plotting of the ungodly will do nothing to change that. He will not neglect the covenant He made with David.[116] The Messiah says, "I will declare the decree: The LORD has said to Me, You are My Son, today I have begotten You. Ask of Me, and I will give You the nations for Your inheritance, and the ends of the earth for Your possession. You shall break them with a rod of iron; You shall dash them to pieces like a potter's vessel" (Psalm 2:7-9).

The idea of the Messiah as the "begotten Son" is an important theme in the New Testament. In some cases the New Testament quotes Psalm 2:7 directly,[117] but there are allusions to Psalm 2:7 as well.[118] If the words of Psalm 2 were ever used in conjunction with the ascension of one of David's descendants to the throne, that merely human king would have, in that context, been considered "the anointed" and the "begotten son." But the purpose for the placement of this psalm in the Psalter is not to preserve ascension formulas, but to point to the ultimate anointed One, the Son of God.

The only wise response for the rulers of the earth is to "be instructed ... serve the LORD with fear, and rejoice with trembling" and to "kiss the Son" (Psalm 2:10-12). They should abandon their vain attempt to rebel and put their trust in the Messiah. If they will abandon their ungodly counsel and meditate in Scripture, this is what they will do.

Psalms 1-2 introduce the contrast between the "righteous" (*tsaddiq*) and the "ungodly" (*rasha*) that continues throughout the Psalter.

The early church saw Psalm 2 as being fulfilled in the actions of Herod, Pontius Pilate, and the unbelieving Gentiles and Jews.[119]

Since Psalms 1-2 function as in introduction to the Book of Psalms, we can expect everything we read from this point forward to reflect on and to build on the themes found in these two psalms. Specifically, we can expect the entire book to continue its focus on the Messiah, whom we know as our Lord and Savior, Jesus Christ, who has come to redeem us from our sins, and who is destined to rule the nations as the King of kings and Lord of lords.[120]

13

The Prayer of Jesus
on the Cross

From noon until 3:00 PM on the day that Jesus was on the cross, there was darkness over all the land. At about 3:00 PM, Jesus, with a loud voice, cried out, "Eli, Eli, lama sabachthani?" In the Aramaic language, Jesus was praying the words of Psalm 22:1. The meaning of these words is, "My God, My God, why have You forsaken me?" (Matthew 27:46).

To read Matthew 27:33-46 and Psalm 22:1-22 together is to see the evident connection between these texts. Psalm 22 has long been viewed as a messianic psalm fulfilled in the sufferings of Jesus on the cross, and this is certainly supported by a reading of Matthew.

Matthew wrote, "Then they crucified Him, and divided his garments, casting lots, that it might be fulfilled which was spoken by the prophet: 'They divided My garments among them, and for My clothing they cast lots'" (Matthew 27:35). The prophet Matthew had in mind was David,[121] who wrote, "They divided My garments among them, and for My clothing they cast lots" (Psalm 22:18).

The crucifixion was accomplished by driving nails through the hands and feet of Jesus to fasten Him to the cross.[122] David wrote, "For dogs have surrounded Me; the congregation of the wicked has enclosed Me. They pierced My hands and My feet" (Psalm 22:16).

Matthew wrote, "And those who passed by blasphemed Him, wagging their heads and saying, 'You who destroy the temple and build it in three days, save Yourself! If You are the Son of God, come down from the cross.' Likewise the chief priests also, mocking with the scribes and elders, said, 'He saved others; Himself He cannot save. If He is the King of Israel, let Him now come down from the cross, and we will believe Him. He trusted in God; let Him deliver Him now, if He will have Him; for He said, "I am the Son of God"'" (Matthew 27:39-43). David wrote, "All those who see Me ridicule Me; they shoot out the lip, they shake the head, saying, 'He trusted in the LORD, let Him rescue Him; let Him deliver Him, since He delights in Him!'" (Psalm 22:7-8).

Matthew wrote, "Now from the sixth hour until the ninth hour there was darkness over all the land" (Matthew 27:45). This means that from noon until 3:00 PM, night interrupted the day. David wrote, "O My God, I cry in the daytime, but You do not hear; and in the night season, and am not silent" (Psalm 22:2).

Matthew wrote, "And about the ninth hour Jesus cried out with a loud voice, saying, 'Eli, Eli, lama sabachthani?' that is, 'My God, My God, why have You forsaken me?'" (Matthew 27:46). David began the psalm, "My God, My God, why have You forsaken me?" (Psalm 22:1).

Another aspect of fulfillment is recognized by John, who wrote, "After this, Jesus, knowing that all things were now accomplished, that the Scripture might be fulfilled, said, 'I thirst!'" (John 19:28). This is an apparent reference to Psalm 22:15, where David wrote, "My strength is dried up like a potsherd, and My tongue clings to My jaws; You have brought me to the dust of death."

Prophetically, in Psalm 22:1-21a the suffering Messiah is speaking, describing His experiences on the cross. In Psalm 22:21b He proclaims that His prayer for deliverance has been answered. We know from the New Testament account that His prayer was answered not by sparing Him from the suffering of the cross, but by the Resurrection. In Psalm 22:22, the Messiah announces His intent to declare the name of the LORD to His brethren and to praise Him in the midst of the assembly.[123] The writer of the Book of Hebrews quoted this verse to show that Jesus is not ashamed to call believers His brothers.[124]

In Psalm 22:23-24, David speaks to the congregation, to those who "fear the LORD," about the suffering of the Messiah.

In Psalm 22:25-27, David speaks to the Messiah.

In Psalm 22:30-31, David looks to the future and declares that the events of Psalm 22 will be recognized to be the work of the LORD by "a people who will be born." This "posterity shall serve Him."[125]

Some have thought that Jesus' plaintive cry, "My God, My God, why have You forsaken me," indicates that at the moment of His greatest need, God abandoned Jesus. This is not the case. Jesus' words indicate instead the genuine depth of the emotional trauma He experienced; His suffering was not just physical; it affected every aspect of His being, materially and immaterially. In the same way that any human being in the midst of the horrors of painful circumstances might cry out, "God, where are you?"[126] so Jesus on the cross cried out of His experience of aloneness and the feeling of being forsaken.

When Jesus uttered the words of Psalm 21:1a, He acknowledged the messianic import of the psalm. Although we have no record that He prayed all of the words in Psalm 22:1-22, we should understand His use of the first words as representative of His entire experience. This is how the psalm was understood by the writers of the Gospels.

Jesus' feeling of being forsaken is further developed in the rest of Psalm 22:1: "Why are You so far from helping Me, and from the words of my groaning?" (verse 1b). Although Jesus prayed, and His prayer was heard,[127] the answer was not to deliver Him from the experience of death. His prayer was answered by means of the Resurrection.[128]

Because the light of day was interrupted by the darkness of night for three hours, from noon until 3:00 PM, Jesus cried out to God "in the daytime" and "in the night season" (verse 2). There was no answer from God at that time; God's answer would come with resurrection.[129]

On the cross Jesus acknowledged the holiness of God, which is demonstrated by His enthronement "in the praises of Israel" (verse 3). The phrase "praises of Israel" is a figure of speech used to confess that God rules between the cherubim on the ark of the covenant.[130] This makes very significant the tearing of the curtain separating the Holy Place from the Most Holy Place in the Jerusalem Temple at the time of Christ's death.[131] The tearing of this veil represented the access into God's presence that is now available to all people of faith on the basis of Christ's death.[132]

In Psalm 22:4-8, the Messiah contrasted His experience on the cross with the experiences of the "fathers" who trusted in God and were delivered (verses 4-5). He prayed, "Our fathers trusted in You; they trusted, and You delivered them. They cried to You, and were delivered; they trusted in You, and were not ashamed" (verses 4-5). When He said, "Our fathers," He acknowledged His solidarity with the people of Israel. This can be attributed to the genuineness and fullness of His human existence. In contrast to those who were delivered, He said, "But I am a worm, and no man; a reproach of men, and despised by the people" (verse 6). The first part of this verse is a figure of speech intended to describe the extent of the reproach Jesus experienced on the cross. His statement, "I am a worm, and no man" is certainly not intended to deny Christ's humanity, any more than it is intended to be literally understood to mean that He is a worm.

The extent of the way the unbelievers despised Jesus can be seen in their ridicule of Him. They denied God had any interest in the events of the Cross. In the Messiah's words, "All those who see Me ridicule Me; they shoot out the lip, they shake the head, saying, 'He trusted in the LORD, let Him rescue Him; let Him deliver Him, since He delights in Him!'" (verses 7-8).

The Messiah acknowledged the genuineness of His human existence and His dependence on God since His birth. He said, "But You are He who took Me out of the womb; you made Me trust while on my mother's breasts. I was cast upon You from birth, from My mother's womb you have been My God" (verses 9-10). The reference to the Messiah's mother is a reference to Mary. Since she was His mother, the Messiah was, by means of the miracle of the Incarnation, a human being. Gabriel said to Mary, "You will conceive in your womb and bring forth a Son, and shall call His name JESUS" (Luke 1:31). Twice in Psalm 22 the Messiah referred to His mother's womb.

The words of verse 11 are similar to those of verse 1b. In verse 11, the Messiah prayed, "Be not far from Me, for trouble is near; for there is none to help." In the last half of verse 1, His words are, "Why are You so far from helping Me, and from the words of My groaning?" Although His prayer was heard, the answer was not deliverance from death. The answer was resurrection from death.

Fierce, wild cattle roamed freely in Bashan, a fertile region east of the Jordan River known for its sheep and plump cattle.[133] The imagery of danger is vividly presented in the words, "Many bulls have surrounded Me; strong bulls of Bashan have encircled Me. They gape at Me with their mouths, like a raging and roaring lion" (verses 12-13).

The Messiah described His physical condition in verses 14-15: "I am poured out like water, and all My bones are out of joint; my heart is like wax; it has melted within Me. My strength is dried up like a potsherd, and My tongue clings to My jaws; you have brought Me to the dust of death." To say he is "poured out like water" and that His heart is like "wax" is a metaphorical way of expressing His formlessness and His inner feelings of anguish; He can no longer function as a human being. Like a dried-out and useless potsherd, a broken piece of pottery, He has exhausted his resilience and is unable to cope with the trauma.[134] On the cross, He cried out, "I thirst" (John 19:28). Not only did Jesus experience dehydration; His bones were out of joint; He was brought "to the dust of death."

The term *dog* was used in a derisive and contemptuous way in the Bible because, although there were domesticated dogs at this time, many packs of scavengers still roamed both inside and outside of the towns.[135] The Messiah's words were, "For dogs have surrounded Me; the congregation of the wicked has enclosed Me. They pierced My hands and My feet" (verse 16).

On the cross, the Messiah endured the shame of nakedness: All of His bones could be counted; the onlookers stared at Him (verse 17).

His garments were divided among those who participated in His crucifixion. They cast lots for His robe (verse 18).[136]

The Messiah's prayer in verses 19-21a recapitulates the danger He faced on the cross: "But You, O LORD, do not be far from Me; O My Strength, hasten to help Me! Deliver Me from the sword, My precious life from the power of the dog. Save Me from the lion's mouth and from the horns of the wild oxen!" (verses 19-21a).

Finally, the sufferings are past. The Messiah declares, "You have answered Me. I will declare Your name to My brethren; in the midst of the assembly I will praise You" (verse 21a-22). The Book of Hebrews sees Psalm 22:21 as being connected with the death of the Messiah and occurring after His death. The phrase "crowned with glory and honor" indicates that this occurred after the Resurrection.[137]

Beginning in Psalm 22:23, David spoke to those who fear the LORD: "You who fear the LORD, praise Him! All you descendants of Jacob, glorify Him, and fear Him, all you offspring of Israel!" This encouragement to praise, glorify, and fear the LORD is due to the fact that the LORD did not despise the Messiah in His afflictions, regardless of the assessment made by those who participated in His crucifixion, nor did He hide His face from the Messiah, even though the Messiah felt forsaken. David wrote, "For He has not despised nor abhorred the affliction of the afflicted; nor has He hidden His face from Him; but when He cried to Him, He heard" (verse 24).

Then, in verse 25, David spoke to the Messiah: "My praise shall be of You in the great assembly; I will pay My vows before those who fear Him."

Verse 26 indicates that the Messiah's victory over death brings blessings for the poor. Those who seek the LORD will have reason to praise Him; their hearts will enjoy abundant life forever.

The death and resurrection of the Messiah will have universal impact. He will be worshiped by "the ends of the world" and "all the families of the nations" (verse 27).

The resurrection of the Messiah further proves the universality and eternality of the rule of the LORD. David wrote, "For the kingdom is the LORD's, and He rules over the nations" (verse 28). In the larger context of Psalms, this is evidence of the certainty of the Davidic Covenant.

Those who will worship the Messiah include the prosperous and the suffering. His rule will be universal. David declared, "All the prosperous of the earth shall eat and worship; all those who go down to the dust shall bow before Him. Even he who cannot keep himself alive" (verse 29).

The worship of the Messiah will not end with the generation who sees the experiences of Psalm 22. He will be served by their posterity. People yet to be born will hear of His righteousness and of the work accomplished on the Cross. As David put it, "A posterity shall serve Him. It will be recounted of the Lord to the next generation, they will come and declare His righteousness to a people who will be born, that He has done this" (verses 30-31).

The Superscription

Since Psalm 22 is a messianic psalm, we would expect the superscription to make some contribution to the messianic theme. The KJV offers a partial translation and transliteration: "To the chief Musician upon Aijeleth Shahar, A Psalm of David." The NKJV offers a translation of Aijeleth Shahar: "To the Chief Musician. Set to 'The Deer of the Dawn.' A Psalm of David." Why, then, does the Septuagint translate the superscription as "For the end, concerning the morning aid, a Psalm of David"?

Kidner's comments are helpful:

> This may be a tune-name ... but is better explained as a glimpse of the theme, and translated ... 'On the help of (*i.e.*, at) daybreak'. The word *'ayyelet* ('Hind', RSV) is very close to the rare word *'eyalut*, 'help' (19, Heb. 20), and could be vocalized to coincide with it, if it is not indeed a feminine form of *'eyal* (help), Psalm 88:4 (Heb. 5). So the title draws attention to the deliverance which will light up the final verses of the psalm.[138]

If this is the way we should read the superscription, the psalm begins by pointing to the resurrection of Christ: It was the Resurrection that was His aid or help on the morning of the first day of the week.[139]

Psalm 22 is not the only Old Testament reference to the events Jesus experienced in His suffering on the cross, but it is certainly a clear and sustained prophecy of the event that brought redemption for the human race. When we see such a finely detailed description of these events in the Hebrew Scriptures, we see the accuracy of Jesus' words: "All things must be fulfilled which were written in the Law of Moses and the Prophets and the Psalms concerning Me" (Luke 24:44). We also see validity of the angel's words to the apostle John: "Worship God! For the testimony of Jesus is the spirit of prophecy" (Revelation 19:10). Prophecy is consumed with the revelation of the Messiah, Jesus Christ.

Although we do not want to read into the text of Scripture something that is not there, neither must we minimize the messianic witness of Scripture. As Paul put it in the third chapter of his second letter to the Corinthians, to read the Old Testament without faith in Christ is to have a veil over one's mind (II Corinthians 3:14). However, "when one turns to the Lord, the veil is taken away. Now the Lord is the Spirit; and where the Spirit of the Lord is, there is liberty" (II Corinthians 3:16-17). Finally, Paul wrote, "But we all, with unveiled face, beholding as in a mirror the glory of the Lord, are being transformed into the same image from glory to glory, just as by the Spirit of the Lord" (II Corinthians 3:18). Like James, Paul compared Scripture to a mirror into which we look. Although all Scripture is given by inspiration of God, Paul at this point was speaking specifically about the Hebrew Scriptures. His point was that as we see the glory of the Lord Jesus in the Hebrew Scriptures, we are transformed into His image by His Spirit. If we do not see Jesus in the Old Testament, we are missing the central message of Scripture. In Paul's words, our minds are blinded. But when we see our Lord there, the Scriptures open up, revealing details about the Messiah, Jesus, that may not even be seen in the New Testament. As we have seen in Psalm 22, the Book of Psalms is a rich resource of this information; to read it as did the writers of the New Testament helps us know our Savior more intimately.

14

Another Prayer of the Messiah

It is widely recognized that when Jesus prayed, "My God, My God, why have You forsaken me," He was praying the words of Psalm 22:1. What may not be so widely recognized is that Psalm 22 is not the only psalm from which He prayed. The Gospels include the words of eleven of Jesus' prayers as well as many other references to Jesus praying without telling us what He prayed. Many of Jesus' prayers are well known to Christians, and they offer valuable insights that can help us know our Lord and Savior more intimately.

It is when we pray that we are most vulnerable, most exposed, and most honest. In our prayers we are not trying to impress anyone or to be someone we are not. As Jesus said, we are not praying to be seen of men.[140] I can clearly remember hearing my grandfather pray. His prayers had a profound influence on me. It was during the Korean War, and I was about five years old. My uncle was in the military. Before my grandfather retired for the evening, he would lift his voice in prayer, asking God to protect those who were in military service for our country. Although I was just a little boy, I can remember that to hear his prayers seemed to usher me into a holy place. Because I was able to hear my grandfather pray, I feel that I knew him more intimately than I would have had I never heard those words. His prayers assured me of his relationship with God and revealed his values. His prayers caused me to think of him not only as a grandfather, but also as a man who knew God and who trusted God with the things he valued most.

Likewise, to hear the prayers of Jesus opens His heart to us in a profound way. On at least one occasion, Jesus specifically pointed out that He prayed in order to increase the faith of those who heard His words. At the tomb of Lazarus, Jesus prayed, "Father, I thank You that You have heard Me. And I know that You always hear Me, but because of the people who are standing by I said this, that they may believe that You sent me" (John 11:41-42).

In addition to the eleven prayers of Jesus that are recorded in the Gospels, it seems possible that other prayers of the Messiah are recorded prophetically in the Book of Psalms. If so, to read these psalms is to obtain an intimate knowledge of Jesus, a knowledge that helps us understand more clearly who He is and what He valued. Jesus was and is God, but He was also a human being who shared in the full range of human experiences. He stood in solidarity with us and, by means of the Scriptures, shares His heart with us in the prayers that are recorded in the pages of the Holy Bible.

In addition to praying the words of Psalm 22:1, and possibly Psalm 22:1-22, on the cross, Jesus also prayed from Psalm 31. Luke records this event: "Now it was about the sixth hour, and there was darkness over all the earth until the ninth hour. Then the sun was darkened, and the veil of the temple was torn in two. And when Jesus had cried out with a loud voice, He said, 'Father, "into Your hands I commit My spirit." ' Having said this, He breathed His last. So when the centurion saw what had happened, he glorified God, saying, 'Certainly this was a righteous Man!' And the whole crowd who came together to that sight, seeing what had been done, beat their breasts and returned. But all His acquaintances, and the women who followed Him from Galilee, stood at a distance, watching these things" (Luke 23:44-49). When Jesus said, "Into Your hands I commit my Spirit," He prayed the words of Psalm 31:5a. The question that immediately arises is whether any of the rest of Psalm 31 should be read as a prayer of the Messiah.

We have seen that Psalm 22:1-22 is a prayer of the Messiah, even though the New Testament records only a portion of Psalm 22:1 being prayed by Jesus on the cross. Is it possible that, like Psalm 22, the entirety or at least a major portion of Psalm 31 forms a messianic prayer, even though Luke records Jesus praying only a portion of verse 5? In view of the fact that there is no change of speakers in Psalm 31, it would be expected that whoever is speaking in verse 5 is speaking throughout the psalm. Since Jesus prayed from verse 5, this means we would read the entire psalm as a messianic prayer, unless there is something elsewhere in the psalm to make that impossible.

Let's examine the possibility the first 22 verses of Psalm 31 form a prayer of the Messiah, with the last two verses of the psalm being the Messiah's admonition to those who believe. To begin, it seems quite clear that Psalm 31:1-5a could be a prayer of the Messiah. This section reads, "In You, O LORD, I put my trust; let me never be ashamed; deliver me in your righteousness. Bow down Your ear to me, deliver me speedily; be my rock of refuge, a fortress of defense to save me. For You are my rock and my fortress; therefore, for Your name's sake, lead me and guide me. Pull me out of the net which they have secretly laid for me, for You are my strength. Into Your hand I commit my spirit" (Psalm 31:1-5a). When we read these words, it is not difficult to imagine them being prayed by Jesus. They sound very much like some of His prayers recorded in the New Testament.

As the psalm opens with the Messiah facing the crucifixion, He puts His trust in the LORD. He prays He will not be ashamed, that is, His trust will not be disappointed, and He will be delivered. This sounds very much like the messianic prayer recorded in Psalm 22:1-5. Notice the similarity of the phrases: "My God, My God, why have You forsaken Me? Why are You so far from helping Me, and from the words of My groaning? O My God, I cry in the daytime, but You do not hear; and in the night season, and am not silent. But You are holy, enthroned in the praises of Israel. Our fathers trusted in You; they trusted, and You delivered them. They cried to You, and were delivered; they trusted in You, and were not ashamed" (Psalm 22:1-5). In Psalm 22, the Messiah recalled how the patriarchs—the fathers—trusted God. In Psalm 31, the Messiah confesses His trust in God. In Psalm 22, the Messiah recalls how God delivered the fathers. In Psalm 31, the Messiah prays for deliverance. In Psalm 22, the Messiah notes the fathers were not ashamed. In Psalm 31, He prays He would never be ashamed.

When we read the Messiah's prayers that are related to His suffering and death, we should note how they are described in the Book of Hebrews: "Who, in the days of His flesh, when He had offered up prayers and supplications, with vehement cries and tears to Him who was able to save Him from death, and was heard because of His godly fear" (Hebrews 5:7). This indicates we should not minimize the agony of His prayers. Whatever the words that may be used, like His cry of forsakenness on the cross, they should not be thought to be too radical for the Messiah to pray: His prayers included vehement cries and tears. We should also not reject the idea that Christ prayed for deliverance from death. The writer of Hebrews said He prayed "to Him who was able to save Him from death." During His prayer in Gethsemane, Jesus said, "O My Father, if it is possible, let this cup pass from Me; nevertheless, not as I will, but as You will" (Matthew 26:39). After waking His sleeping disciples, Jesus returned and prayed a second time, "O My Father, if this cup cannot pass away from Me unless I drink it, Your will be done" (Matthew 26:42). Matthew pointed out that during this time of prayer, Jesus was sorrowful and deeply distressed.[141] The Book of Hebrews tells us the prayers of Jesus were heard. This does not mean He was spared from death; it means He conquered death by the Resurrection.

In Psalm 31:2, the Messiah prays that His deliverance would be speedy. This is in harmony with Psalm 22:19, where He prays, "But You, O LORD, do not be far from Me; O My Strength, hasten to help Me!"

In Psalm 31:4, the Messiah asks to be pulled from the net secretly laid for Him. In the Gospel of John, we discover that unbelievers sought to kill Jesus, even before the time of His crucifixion.[142]

As we have already seen, Psalm 31:5a is definitely a prayer of the Messiah; Jesus prayed these words on the cross: "Into Your hand I commit my spirit." It was Jesus, not those who crucified Him or the devil, who was in charge on the cross. He did not die until He yielded up His spirit.[143] And He yielded up His spirit before the soldiers could break His legs to hasten his death, in fulfillment of Psalm 34:20: "Not one of His bones shall be broken" (John 19:36). Jesus foretold the control He would exercise over His death in one of His prayers: "Therefore My Father loves Me, because I lay down My life that I may take it again. No one takes it from Me, but I lay it down of Myself. I have power to lay it down, and I have power to take it again. This command I have received from My Father" (John 10:17-18).

Psalm 31:6 describes the Messiah's hatred of idolatry and reaffirms His trust in the Lord, which was first declared in the first verse of the psalm.

In Psalm 31:7-8, the Messiah rejoices in the Lord's mercy and that His trouble has been considered and His soul known in adversities. The prayer says, "I will be glad and rejoice in Your mercy, for You have considered my trouble; You have known my soul in adversities, and have not shut me up into the hand of the enemy; You have set my feet in a wide place." Again it is not difficult to imagine this as a prayer of the Messiah. These words are conceptually quite similar to some of the prayers of Jesus recorded in the New Testament or to other messianic prayers recorded in the psalms.

Psalm 31:9-10a form a plea for mercy by One who is in trouble, whose material and immaterial parts waste away with grief. He prays, "Have mercy on me, O LORD, for I am in trouble; My eye wastes away with grief, yes, my soul and my body! For my life is spent with grief, and my years with sighing." These words remind us of the description of the Messiah found in Isaiah 53:3, 10, 12: "He is ... a man of sorrows and acquainted with grief ... Yet it pleased the LORD to bruise Him; He has put Him to grief ... He poured out His soul unto death."

In Psalm 31:11 the Messiah describes Himself as a reproach among His enemies and His neighbors and as so repulsive to His acquaintances that they flee from Him. Let's compare this with a variety of other Scriptures concerning the Messiah. First, Isaiah 53:3 reads, "He is despised and rejected by men ... and we hid, as it were, our faces from Him; He was despised, and we did not esteem Him." Second, Psalm 22:6-7a reads, "But I am a worm, and no man; a reproach of men, and despised by the people. All those who see me ridicule Me." Third, we should note that when Jesus was arrested in Gethsemane, "all the disciples forsook Him and fled" (Matthew 26:56).

In Psalm 31:12 the Messiah describes Himself as "forgotten like a dead man, out of mind ... a broken vessel." Similarly, in Psalm 22:15, the Messiah prays, "You have brought Me to the dust of death." In the messianic prophecy of Isaiah 53, we read, "He was cut off from the land of the living ... and they made His grave with the wicked ... He poured out His soul unto death" (Isaiah 53:8-9, 12).

In Psalm 31:13 the Messiah recounts the slander and fear accompanying the plans of those who would take

His life. He says, "For I hear the slander of many; fear is on every side; while they take counsel together against me, they scheme to take away my life." The same idea is expressed in the poetic language of Psalm 22:12-13: "Many bulls have surrounded Me; strong bulls of Bashan have encircled Me. They gape at Me with their mouths, like a raging and roaring lion." Several New Testament verses are connected with this idea. When Jesus was staying with His disciples in Galilee, He said to them, "The Son of Man is about to be betrayed into the hands of men, and they will kill Him, and the third day He will be raised up" (Matthew 17:22-23). The death of Jesus is foretold several times in the Gospels.[144]

In Psalm 31:14 the Messiah reaffirms His trust in the LORD for the second time.

In the next verse the Messiah confesses His life is in the hand of the LORD and prays for deliverance from His enemies who persecute Him (Psalm 31:15). This is very much like His prayer recorded in Psalm 22:20-21: "Deliver Me ... from the power of the dog. Save Me from the lion's mouth and from the horns of the wild oxen!"

In Psalm 31:16 the Messiah prays that God's face would shine upon Him and that He would be saved, or delivered. He identifies Himself as the servant of the LORD, as He is identified in the messianic prophecy of Isaiah 52:13.

As in the first verse of the psalm, the Messiah prays in Psalm 31:17 that He would not be ashamed. In other words, He prays His trust in the LORD would be vindicated.

In Psalm 31:18 the Messiah prays that lying lips would be put to silence. This is a reference to those who "speak insolent things proudly and contemptuously against the righteous." This anticipates Matthew 26:59-61: "Now the chief priests, the elders, and all the council sought false testimony against Jesus to put Him to death, but found none. Even though many false witnesses came forward, they found none. But at last two false witnesses came forward and said, 'This fellow said, "I am able to destroy the temple of God and to build it in three days.""'"

In Psalm 31:19 the Messiah testifies to the greatness of the goodness of the LORD to those who fear and trust Him. This reference to trust in the LORD recapitulates the references to trust in verses 1, 6, and 14. The reference to fearing the LORD picks up the same idea in Psalm 22, where the Messiah prays, "You who fear the LORD, praise Him! All you descendants of Jacob, glorify Him, and fear Him, all you offspring of Israel!" (Psalm 22:23).

In the next verse, the Messiah acknowledges the LORD will hide those who fear Him and trust Him in His secret place, "a pavilion" (Psalm 31:20). This is a reference to the Temple of the LORD.

In Psalm 31:21 the Messiah blesses the LORD for His marvelous kindness "in a strong city." This seems to be a reference to the future restoration of Jerusalem and the Temple, as seen in references to the "secret place" and the "pavilion" in the previous verse.

In the final words of this prayer, the Messiah acknowledges He spoke with haste when He said He was "cut off" from the eyes of the LORD, and He confesses the LORD heard His prayer (Psalm 31:22). This is quite similar to the Messiah's prayer in Psalm 22:1-2, 21: "My God, My God, why have You forsaken Me? Why are You so far from helping Me, and from the words of My groaning? ... You have answered Me."

205

We can see everything we have read so far from Psalm 31 can be understood prophetically as a prayer of the Messiah. Indeed, Jesus did pray the words of verse 5a on the cross. But there are two portions of this psalm we have not read, and it may seem at first that they prevent this psalm from being a messianic prayer. First, verse 5b reads, "You have redeemed me, O LORD God of truth." How can this be a prayer of the Messiah? The Messiah is the Redeemer; He does not need redemption. But this problem is removed when we realize the Hebrew word *padah*, translated "redeemed" by some English translations, contains within its range of meaning the idea of "rescue." One translation renders the verse, "I entrust my spirit into your hand. Rescue me, LORD, for you are a faithful God."[145] If this is a plea for rescue, it fits within the context of the prayers of Jesus in the Garden of Gethsemane and on the cross.

The greater problem, however, may seem to be the second half of verse 10, which reads, "My strength fails because of my iniquity, and my bones waste away." The reference to the effect of suffering on the Messiah's bones reminds us of Psalm 22:14, where the Messiah says, "All My bones are out of joint." But we know the Messiah had no sin, so how can the statement, "My strength fails because of my iniquity" be a messianic prayer? Again, the solution can be found in the range of meaning of the Hebrew word translated "iniquity" by some English translations. The word is `*avon*, and it contains within its range of meaning the idea of punishment or ruin. One translation, for example, renders the verse, "My life is consumed by anguish and my years by groaning; my strength fails because of my affliction, and my bones grow weak."[146]

Other translations render the verse, "For my life is spent with sorrow, and my years with sighing; my strength fails because of my misery, and my bones waste away."[147] But perhaps most thought provoking is the translation found in the Septuagint, which was relied on so much by the writers of the New Testament. This Greek translation, completed before the time of Christ and quoted by Him, renders Psalm 31:9, "For my life is spent with grief, and my years with groanings; my strength has been weakened through poverty, and my bones are troubled." This graphic description of suffering can be clearly understood as a reference to the Messiah. Paul wrote, "For you know the grace of our Lord Jesus Christ, that though He was rich, yet for your sakes He became poor, that you through His poverty might become rich" (II Corinthians 8:9).

Not only is there nothing to prevent us from reading Psalm 31 as a prayer of the Messiah; there is every indication that it is indeed a prophetic anticipation of the prayers of Jesus. We know for certain Jesus did pray from this psalm during His sufferings on the cross. By reading this psalm, we can, in a very real sense, listen in on Jesus' words during the time of His greatest vulnerability and agony. By reading His words, we know our Savior more intimately.

In addition we are challenged and encouraged by the two closing verses of the psalm, immediately after the conclusion of the Messiah's prayer. They read: "O, love the LORD, all you His saints! For the LORD preserves the faithful, and fully repays the proud person. Be of good courage, and He shall strengthen your heart, all you who hope in the LORD" (Psalm 31:23-24). The Messiah's admonition arises out of His experience with suffering and the discovery that God is with us in the most difficult and trying circumstances and that He does answer prayer and rescue us, in His own time.

Psalm 31 shows us that the Messiah's experiences on the cross can be an example of how we should love the LORD, be faithful, and be courageous, with the kind of courage that arises from hope. We could almost imagine that the apostle Paul was reading the last two verses of Psalm 31 when he wrote the immortal words, "And now abide faith, hope, love, these three; but the greatest of these is love" (I Corinthians 13:13).

In the final analysis, the good life is life lived with faith in God, love for God and other people, and the assured hope that God will keep every promise He has made. This is what the Messiah tells us—it is what He found to be true as He went through the darkest valley of life. In the words of Psalm 23, located between the clearly messianic Psalms 22 and 31, we discover these profound words: "Yea, though I walk through the valley of the shadow of death, I will fear no evil; for You are with me; Your rod and Your staff, they comfort me. You prepare a table before me in the presence of my enemies; You anoint my head with oil; my cup runs over. Surely goodness and mercy shall follow me all the days of my life; and I will dwell in the house of the LORD forever."

Conclusion

In the previous chapters we have been looking into the Old Testament to discover its witness to the Messiah, Jesus Christ. To use a well-known term in literature, we might say we have been "reading between the lines." But as we all know, this term does not imply we have been reading something into the text; instead, we have been reading the text more closely than we may have read it before. To say that we are reading the text closely means that we are looking for verbal links within and between the various books of the Bible. It also means we are paying attention even to the order of the books or to the components within the books, like the psalms, in an effort to discern the interpretive influence of these arrangements. Finally, to read the text closely means we are sensitive even to the similarity of grammatical structures within or between biblical books. Since we believe every word of Scripture is given by inspiration of God, all of these concerns are valid, important, and even essential to correct interpretation of Scripture.

The Use of the Old Testament in the New Testament

Perhaps the first thing that strikes us as we look for verbal links between the various books of the Bible is the phenomenon of verbal links between the testaments.

Since we believe the writers of the New Testament were inspired in their use of the Old Testament, these links are important to help us understand the meaning of the Hebrew Scriptures. For our present purposes, they are important to help us understand the christology of the Old Testament, which is another way of referring to the messianic focus of the Hebrew Bible.

The New Testament quotes, paraphrases, or alludes to the Old Testament nearly eight hundred times. By my count, it is precisely 787 times.[148] It is interesting to note how this total number breaks down among the various books of the Old Testament.

Book	Number of references in NT	Book	Number of references in NT
Gen	70	Isa	165
Exod	75	Jer	25
Lev	22	Ezek	6
Num	7	Dan	15
Deut	94	Hos	13
Josh	1	Joel	8
I Sam	4	Amos	5
II Sam	6	Jonah	3
I Kgs	5	Mic	5
II Kgs	2	Nah	2
Neh	1	Hab	6
Job	3	Hag	1
Pss	206	Zech	11
Prov	18	Mal	8

The New Testament quotes, alludes to, or paraphrases material from twenty-eight of the Old Testament books. There are eleven Old Testament books not referred to in the New Testament. Each of the three sections of the Hebrew Bible is, however, well represented in the New Testament. The Law is referred to 268 times in the New Testament, the Prophets 215 times, and the Psalms (also known as the Writings) 304 times. Within each of these sections, Deuteronomy is most frequently referenced from the Law, with ninety-four quotes, allusions, or paraphrases in the New Testament; Isaiah is most frequently referenced from the Prophets, with 165 quotes, allusions, or paraphrases in the New Testament; Psalms is most frequently referenced from the section known as the Psalms or Writings, with 206 quotes, allusions, or paraphrases in the New Testament.

When we look at the four Gospels, we discover Matthew quotes from, alludes to, or paraphrases the Old Testament sixty-six times, Mark thirty-four times, Luke forty-two times, and John twenty times. Each reference from the Old Testament in Matthew but one is either about Jesus or used by Jesus. In the one exception, a Sadducee quotes from the Old Testament while questioning Jesus. In Mark, every reference from the Old Testament but two is either about Jesus or used by Jesus. In the two exceptions, the Old Testament is quoted from by someone questioning Jesus. In Luke, every reference from the Hebrew Scriptures but two is either about Jesus or used by Jesus. In one of the two, the Old Testament is quoted by someone questioning Jesus; in the other exception, the disciples refer to the Old Testament in a misguided effort to justify calling fire down from heaven on the Samaritans. In John, each reference from the Old Testament but one is either about Jesus or used by Him. In the one exception, the Old Testament is quoted by someone in a conversation with Jesus.

From this brief survey we can see the significance of reading the Hebrew Scriptures carefully to discover their christology. If we believe the New Testament is inspired equally with the Old Testament, we must believe the use of Old Testament references in the New Testament accurately represents the intent and meaning of the Hebrew Scriptures. The doctrine of inspiration does not allow the writers of the New Testament to be mistaken in their use of the Old Testament or to be guilty of reading meaning into the Hebrew Scriptures that is not there.

An Example: Matthew Reads Hosea; Hosea Reads Numbers

If it seems that the New Testament is creative in its use of Old Testament references—in other words, if it seems that the New Testament is reading meaning into the Hebrew Scriptures—this should prompt us to read the Old Testament more closely. For example, when Matthew interprets Hosea 11:1 as being fulfilled in the trip of Joseph, Mary, and the young child Jesus to Egypt, we may at first question Matthew's reading of Hosea. An angel of the Lord had appeared to Joseph in a dream, saying, "Arise, take the young Child and His mother, flee to Egypt, and stay there until I bring you word; for Herod will seek the young Child to destroy Him" (Matthew 2:13). Matthew records that Joseph took Jesus and His mother and departed for Egypt during the night. Then Matthew wrote they were there "until the death of Herod, that it might be fulfilled which was spoken by the Lord through the prophet, saying, 'Out of Egypt I called My Son'" (Matthew 2:15). The Scripture to which Matthew referred was Hosea 11:1: "When Israel was a child, I loved him, and out of Egypt I called My son." If we had never read Matthew's use of this verse, we might assume that that words "My son" here refer to Israel as a nation. Then, we would probably think the only thing in view in Hosea was the Exodus of Israel from Egypt.

One solution to this dilemma is to suggest there is a double reference in Hosea. Some think that Matthew was "spiritualizing" Hosea. These ideas open up the entire Old Testament to the question of double or multiple meanings, although it is suggested by some that such flexibility of meaning is possible only where the New Testament reads the Hebrew Scripture in this creative way.

But there is another possibility; perhaps a closer reading of the Old Testament will show that Matthew's understanding of Hosea is the literal meaning intended by Hosea. In this case, Hosea 11:1 is a messianic prophecy that actually anticipates the trip into Egypt taken by the holy family for the protection of the child Jesus, making it necessary for them to be called out of Egypt at the death of Herod. This possibility provokes us to examine the intertextuality between the prophecies of Hosea and Balaam. We have already seen that Balaam uttered profound and detailed prophecies about the Messiah.[149]

In a prophetic statement that is unquestionably about the Messiah, Balaam said, "God brings him out of Egypt; He has strength like a wild ox; He shall consume the nations, his enemies; He shall break their bones and pierce them with his arrows. He bows down, he lies down as a lion; and as a lion, who shall rouse him?" (Numbers 24:8-9). It is important to note Balaam's prophecies are described as parables.[150] By definition a parable places two things side by side for purposes of comparison. In the case of this point of Balaam's prophecy, Israel's Exodus from Egypt is compared to the Messiah's Exodus from Egypt, just as the Messiah is compared to a wild ox in His ability to conquer the nations and to a lion as he lies down after consuming his prey. Later in Balaam's prophecy the Messiah is compared to a star and a scepter.[151] Balaam offered an inspired interpretation of the christological significance of Israel's Exodus from Egypt, an historical event with profound metaphorical implications. This should not be surprising in view of the fact that the Passover, an integral part of the Exodus event, is clearly proclaimed in the New Testament to have messianic meaning. The parabolic use of Israel's Exodus is understood by Hosea, who had access to the Pentateuch and who could read Balaam's christological interpretation of the Exodus event. Thus, when Hosea wrote, "And out of Egypt I called My son," he endorsed Balaam's statement, "God brings him out of Egypt" (Numbers 24:8). Further, just as Balaam's prophecies were in the form of parables, so Hosea wrote, "I have also spoken by the prophets, and have multiplied visions; I have given symbols through the witness of the prophets" (Hosea 12:10).

As Matthew understood in his quote from Hosea, the historical event of Israel's Exodus was itself a prophetic foreshadowing of a greater Exodus yet to come. This greater Exodus was not just the deliverance of a nation of people from political oppression; it would be the deliverance of mankind from slavery to sin. This deliverance did not involve a nation's trek from Egypt, but a divinely ordained journey of the young Messiah from Egypt back to the land God had promised to Abraham, Isaac, and Jacob.

To read the text this way is not to spiritualize the Old Testament or to assume double meanings. It is to interpret the text the way the writers of Scriptures themselves interpreted earlier texts and the way those texts were intended to be interpreted in their original shape. This demonstrates the idea of intertextuality.

Paul Reads Exodus

In the meantime, since the Pentateuch should be viewed as one book, Balaam's use of Israel's Exodus to represent the Messiah's trip from Egypt to Israel is an example of inner-textuality; it is an interpretive use of an earlier text within the same book.[152] The story of the Exodus is included in the Pentateuch not merely to provide an account of Israel's history, but to serve as a backdrop for the continually unfolding drama of God's redemptive purposes. This drama would come to its fullness and completion in the person of Jesus Christ and His death, burial, and resurrection. For example, in an extended treatment of the theological significance of Israel's Exodus from Egypt, Paul wrote, "Moreover, brethren, I do not want you to be unaware that all our fathers were under the cloud, all passed through the sea, all were baptized into Moses in the cloud and in the sea, all ate the same spiritual food, and all drank the same spiritual drink. For they drank of that spiritual Rock that followed them, and that Rock was Christ. But with most of them God was not well pleased, for their bodies were scattered in the wilderness. Now these things became our examples, to the intent that we should not lust after evil things as they also lusted. And do not become idolaters as were some of them. As it is written, 'The people sat down to eat and drink, and rose up to play.' Nor let us commit sexual immorality, as some of them did, and in one day twenty-three thousand fell; nor let us tempt Christ, as some of them also tempted, and were destroyed by serpents; nor complain, as some of them also complained, and were destroyed by the destroyer. Now all these things happened to them as examples, and they were written for our admonition, upon whom the ends of the ages have come" (I Corinthians 10:1-11).

In this text it is clear there is a correlation between the church and the ancient Israelites. First, even though the church in Corinth consisted primarily of Gentile believers, Paul referred to "all our fathers." There was a sense in which first-century Gentile Christians could claim the ancient Israelites as their ancestors. This sense becomes clear as we proceed through Paul's points of comparison; the connection is spiritual. The Israelites were baptized into Moses. This baptism involved the cloud, which was a visible representation of God's presence with the Israelites, and the sea, which served as Israel's path of escape from the Egyptians and which also resulted in the destruction of their enemies. Christians, meanwhile, are baptized into Jesus Christ, who can be said to be the new Moses who leads us to deliverance. This baptism involves the Holy Spirit, which is God among and within us, and water, which is connected with the remission of our sins.[153] In the prophetic view of the law, Jesus, the

216

Messiah, is the Prophet like Moses who is raised up from among His brethren and whose voice must be heard.[154]

Further, Paul said that all of our fathers ate the same spiritual food and drank the same spiritual drink. They did this when they drank of the spiritual Rock that followed them; that Rock was Christ. Here we discover that the manna that fell from heaven to satisfy the Israelite's hunger and the water that flowed from the rock smitten by Moses represented something far beyond physical food and drink. We learn in the New Testament that Christ was the true Bread from heaven and that to believe on Jesus is to receive living, or life-giving, water. Some of those who questioned Jesus asked, "What sign will You perform then, that we may see it and believe You? What work will You do? Our fathers ate the manna in the desert; as it is written, 'He gave them bread from heaven to eat'" (John 6:30-31). Notice how these questioners, like Paul, referred to the fathers. Unlike Paul, however, they did not understand that the experiences of the fathers foretold a greater future reality. Instead, they looked for a repeat of the same kind of experiences. Jesus answered, "Most assuredly, I say to you, Moses did not give you the bread from heaven, but My Father gives you the true bread from heaven. For the bread of God is He who comes down from heaven and gives life to the world" (John 6:32-33). Jesus distinguished between the manna and the true bread. The manna was not the true bread; it merely represented true Bread yet to come.

Those who heard Jesus said, "Lord, give us this bread always" (John 6:34). Jesus answered, "I am the bread of life. He who comes to Me shall never hunger, and he who believes in Me shall never thirst" (John 6:35). As

Paul pointed out, the bread and water enjoyed by the ancient Israelites have spiritual counterparts for us. This does not mean that we are to interpret the Old Testament "spiritually," or in such a way as to deny the literal reality of the events recorded there. Instead we are to read the Old Testament as did the writers of the New Testament: the events found in the Hebrew Scriptures anticipate and represent greater realities that will be brought to light in the messianic age, with the coming of Jesus Christ.

From Paul we learn this illustrative function of the Old Testament is not limited to the positive representation of the redemption that is found in Christ; it includes warnings and rebukes based upon the experiences of our fathers. Paul wrote, "Nor let us tempt Christ, as some of them also tempted, and were destroyed by serpents" (I Corinthians 10:9). This recalls the event of the bronze serpent. Here is the record of this episode in Israel's history: "Then they journeyed from Mount Hor by the Way of the Red Sea, to go around the land of Edom; and the soul of the people became very discouraged on the way. And the people spoke against God and against Moses: 'Why have you brought us up out of Egypt to die in the wilderness? For there is no food and no water, and our soul loathes this worthless bread.' So the LORD sent fiery serpents among the people, and they bit the people; and many of the people of Israel died. Therefore the people came to Moses, and said, 'We have sinned, for we have spoken against the LORD and against you; pray to the LORD that He take away the serpents from us.' So Moses prayed for the people. Then the LORD said to Moses, 'Make a fiery serpent, and set it on a pole; and it shall be that everyone who is bitten, when he looks at it, shall live.'

So Moses made a bronze serpent, and put it on a pole; and so it was, if a serpent had bitten anyone, when he looked at the bronze serpent, he lived" (Numbers 21:4-9).

Jesus Reads Numbers

If we did not have the New Testament, we might read this story as simply an interesting event in Israel's history. But Paul, based on this event, warned the Corinthians not to tempt Christ, the Messiah. Paul's warning becomes even more compelling when we read how Jesus Himself interpreted the meaning of this event. Jesus said, "And as Moses lifted up the serpent in the wilderness, even so must the Son of Man be lifted up, that whoever believes in Him should not perish but have eternal life. For God so loved the world that He gave His only begotten Son, that whoever believes in Him should not perish but have everlasting life" (John 3:14-16). Neither Paul nor Jesus were reading a meaning into the Old Testament story of the bronze serpent. Instead, the event itself was intended from the beginning to be read as a prophetic anticipation of the messianic age. We know this is true because Paul concluded his extended treatment of Israel's history with these words: "Now all these things happened to them as examples, and they were written for our admonition, upon whom the ends of the ages have come" (I Corinthians 10:11).

The Old Testament Is Our Book

So when we read the Old Testament, it is not just that we have discovered an interesting book with lots of stories from which we can draw moral teachings. Instead, the events happened as examples to us; they were intended to foreshadow future messianic realities even as they were occurring. Nor, according to Paul, was the Old Testament written merely to preserve the history of Israel. Instead, it was written for our admonition, upon whom the ends of the ages have come. This means there is no future age that will transcend this age and render it irrelevant. We are living in the end of the ages; we are living in the era anticipated by the Hebrew Scriptures, the messianic age.

Peter put this clearly in his first letter: "Of this salvation the prophets have inquired and searched carefully, who prophesied of the grace that would come to you, searching what, or what manner of time, the Spirit of Christ who was in them was indicating when He testified beforehand the sufferings of Christ and the glories that would follow. To them it was revealed that, not to themselves, but to us they were ministering the things which now have been reported to you through those who have preached the gospel to you by the Holy Spirit sent from heaven—things which angels desire to look into" (I Peter 1:10-12).

When we read the Hebrew Scriptures, let's read them with a keen awareness of their testimony of our Lord and Savior, Jesus Christ. As we note the connections between the testaments and even the connections between earlier and later texts in the Old Testament, we will have an opportunity to grow in the grace and knowledge of our Lord and Savior, Jesus Christ.[155] This is the ultimate goal of our Christian life.

Endnotes

[1] II Peter 3:18.

[2] Acts 17:6.

[3] Luke 24:33-35.

[4] Luke 24:36-37.

[5] Luke 24:41-43.

[6] Compare Luke 24:49 with Acts 1:8.

[7] See also Acts 26:26.

[8] Other terms are sometimes used to express these ideas.

[9] *http://bible-researcher.com/aramaic4.html.* Accessed April 2, 2007.

[10] Ibid.

[11] Genesis 2:19-20.

[12] Luke 3:23-38.

[13] See Ray Summers, *Essentials of New Testament Greek* (rev. by Thomas Sawyer; Nashville: Broadman and Holman, 1995), 121.

[14] Luke 24:44.

[15] Deuteronomy 6:16.

[16] Genesis 5:5.

[17] Genesis 3:22-24.

[18] The NKJV translates `*iyroh* "his donkey." The KJV translates "his foal." Regardless of the translation, the only two places in the Old Testament where "colt" and "foal" (or donkey) are found together are Genesis 49:11 and Zechariah 9:9.

[19] Luke 24:44.

[20] I Samuel 8:7.

[21] See Matthew 1:2-6; Luke 3:32-34.

[22] See John H. Sailhamer, *The Expositor's Bible Commentary*, vol. 2 (Frank E. Gaebelein, gen. ed.; Grand Rapids: Zondervan, 1990), 276-277.

[23] See Exodus 12:4-11.

[24] Compare Exodus 12:6 with Exodus 12:15-20, noting especially v. 18. See also Exodus 13:3-10.

[25] Revelation 5:11.

[26] Revelation 19:11-20.

[27] Acts 8:38.

[28] Numbers 24:17.

[29] Acts 15:1-6.

[30] John 1:19-21.

[31] Luke 24:44.

[32] Luke 24:44.

[33] II Peter 3:18.

[34] Acts 3:26.

[35] In the Hebrew Scriptures, I and II Samuel form one book, as do I and II Kings.

[36] See Ezekiel 34:11-31; 37:15-28.

[37] Revelation 21:22.

[38] See Isaiah 1:9-10.

[39] Ezra 3:12.

[40] Isaiah 11:1-10.

[41] Exodus 6:3.

[42] John 12:37.

[43] Deuteronomy 22:20-24.

[44] Isaiah 7:11.

[45] I Timothy 3:16; John 1:14.

[46] See Luke 4:16-21.

[47] See also Isaiah 29:18-19.

[48] John 1:29, 36.

[49] Matthew 8:14-16; Mark 1:32-34; Luke 4:40-41.

[50] Luke 4:41.

[51] New Living Translation (Wheaton, Ill.: Tyndale House Publishers, Inc., 1996).

[52] Isaiah 53:7.

[53] Isaiah 53:9.

[54] Luke 4:28-29.

[55] C. S. Lewis, *Mere Christianity* (New York: Macmillan Publishing, 1976), 56.

[56] Matthew 2:1-11.

[57] Isaiah 60:6.

[58] Isaiah 6:1-3.

[59] Acts 1:5.

[60] See Joel 1:5, 10; 2:24; 3:18.

[61] Acts 2:13.

[62] F. F. Bruce, *Commentary on the Book of the Acts* (Grand Rapids: Wm. B. Eerdmans, 1977), 69.

[63] See Graham S. Ogden, *A Promise of Hope—A Call to Obedience: A Commentary on the Books of Joel and Malachi*, International Theological Commentary (Grand Rapids: Eerdmans Publishing Company, 1987), 38; John Barton, *Joel and Obadiah: A Commentary*, Old Testament Library (Louisville, Ky.: Westminster John Knox Press, 2001), 98; David Allan Hubbard, *Joel and Amos*, Tyndale Old Testament Commentaries (Downers Grove, Ill.: InterVarsity Press, 1990), 71; S. R. Driver, *Joel and Amos: With Introduction and Notes*, (Cambridge: The University Press, 1897), 66.

[64] Matthew 24:6-7.

[65] See Rom 15:8-9; Ps 18:49.

[66] See also Luke 24:25-27; II Corinthians 3:14-17.

[67] See Matthew 22:46 and Mark 12:34-37; Luke 20:34-40.

[68] See Acts 2:29-31; II Samuel 7:12; Psalm 132:11.

[69] Although it is common to reject the superscriptions of the Psalms as being of later origin and uninspired, they are actually included in the Hebrew text as the first verse of the psalm. See II Samuel 23:1-2; Acts 1:15-16.

[70] See Hebrews 1:10-12; Psalm 102:25-27.

[71] See I Timothy 3:16; John 1:14.

[72] See Hebrews 2:5-9.

[73] See also Matthew 21:33-46; Mark 12:1-11; Luke 20:9-19; Romans 9:33; Ephesians 2:20; I Peter 2:4, 7.

[74] See Matthew 21:9; Mark 11:9; Luke 19:38-40. The Hebrew words translated "save now" are transliterated "hosanna."

[75] See Earl D. Radmacher, gen. ed., *The Nelson Study Bible* (Nashville: Thomas Nelson Publishers, 1997), 1822.

[76] See Galatians 1:11-12, 15-18; 2:1-10.

[77] See Psalm 89:20.

[78] See also Acts 13:29.

[79] Compare Acts 13:36-37; 2:29-35.

[80] See Psalm 117:1; Romans 15:9, 12.

[81] See Hebrews 2:6-8.

[82] See I Corinthians 15:3-8, 12-30.

[83] Hebrews 2:1-3; Acts 7:38; Galatians 3:19.

[84] Acts 4:24-28.

[85] The NKJV indicates that the Son, the Messiah, is Yahweh by use of capital letters (LORD). The Book of Hebrews quotes the Septuagint translation of Psalm 102, which reads "Lord" in verse 25 (verse 26 in the Septuagint) due to the fact that the entire psalm is addressed to Yahweh (see superscription and verse 1).

[86] Matthew 22:44-46.

[87] Acts 2:34-35.

[88] F. F. Bruce, *The Epistle to the Hebrews, The New International Commentary on the New Testament* (Grand Rapids, MI: Wm. B. Eerdmans, 1964), 7.

[89] I Timothy 3:16.

[90] See Hebrews 1:2-3; Revelation 11:15.

[91] I Corinthians 15:24-26; Hebrews 10:13.

[92] Genesis 14:18-20; Hebrews 7:1-22.

[93] Luke 24:44.

[94] Acts 4:24-27.

[95] Acts 13:33.

[96] Hebrews 1:5; 5:5.

[97] Revelation 19:8.

[98] See Psalm 4:6; 18:28; 27:1; 30:5; 36:9; 37:6.

[99] See Psalm 7:6; 9:7-8, 16; 25:9; 33:5; 35:23; 37:6, 28; 72:2.

[100] The Hebrew phrase transliterates as *meshiyach 'elohey ya'akov*.

[101] See the discussion in John H. Sailhamer, *Introduction to Old Testament Theology: A Canonical Approach* (Grand Rapids: Zondervan Publishing House, 1995), 132-142.

[102] See Bruce K. Waltke, "A Canonical Process Approach to the Psalms," in *Tradition and Testament: Essays in Honor of Charles Lee Feinberg* (John S. and Paul D. Feinberg, eds.; Chicago: Moody Press, 1981), 3-18 and Philip E. Satterthwaite, Richard S. Hess, and Gordon J. Wenham, *The Lord's Anointed: Interpretations of Old Testament Messianic Texts* (Grand Rapids: Baker Publishing Group, 1995).

[103] See II Samuel 7:4-16; I Kings 6:11-13; 11:9-13; Isaiah 55:1-4; Luke 1:32-33; Acts 2:30-36; Psalm 132:10-18.

[104] See Acts 2:25-31.

[105] The superscription is the first verse in the Hebrew text.

[106] Sailhamer, *Introduction to Old Testament Theology*, 204-05 and *NIV Compact Bible Commentary*, 247-248.

[107] Acts 2:25-36.

[108] Psalm 19:7-8.

[109] Psalm 20:6.

[110] See Psalm 119:1 (the word "law" appears in Psalm 119 twenty-five times).

[111] Psalms 120-134.

[112] See Psalm 132:10-18.

[113] The discussion of the themes in Psalms 1-2 follows John H. Sailhamer, *NIV Compact Bible Commentary* (Grand Rapids: Zondervan Publishing House, 1994), 315.

[114] "Egyptian kings celebrated their rule by writing the names of their enemies on pots and symbolically smashing them. These are referred to as the execration texts. Assyrian kings likewise used the metaphor of smashed pottery to assert their supremacy over enemies." John H. Walton, Victor H. Matthews, Mark W. Chavalas, *The IVP Bible Background Commentary, Old Testament* (Downers Grove, Ill.: InterVarsity Press, 2000), 519.

[115] See Psalm 1:6; 2:12.

[116] See II Samuel 7:8-17; Psalm 89:34-37.

[117] Acts 13:33; Hebrews 1:5; 5:5.

[118] John 1:14, 18; 3:16, 18; I John 4:9.

[119] See Acts 4:24-28.

[120] Revelation 19:15-16.

[121] See Acts 2:29-30.

[122] See Luke 24:39-40; John 20:25, 27.

¹²³ In this case, the "name" of the LORD represents the works of the LORD in raising the Messiah from the dead.

¹²⁴ Hebrews 2:11-12.

¹²⁵ The broad outline of Psalm 22 presented here follows Sailhamer, *NIV Compact Bible Commentary*, 319.

¹²⁶ See Psalm 10:1.

¹²⁷ Hebrews 5:7.

¹²⁸ Notice the contextual connection between the death of Jesus and the words of Psalm 22:22 in Hebrews 2:9-12.

¹²⁹ Romans 1:4.

¹³⁰ Willem A. VanGemeren, *The Expositor's Bible Commentary*, vol. 5 (Frank E. Gaebelein, gen. ed.; Grand Rapids: Zondervan, 1991), 201. See Psalms 80:1; 99:1.

¹³¹ Matthew 27:51.

¹³² See Hebrews 10:19-22.

¹³³ Walton, Matthews, and Chavalas, 523.

¹³⁴ VanGemeren, 205.

¹³⁵ Walton, Matthews, and Chavalas, 524.

¹³⁶ Matthew 27:35.

¹³⁷ See Hebrews 2:9-12.

¹³⁸ Derek Kidner, *Psalms 1-72* (Downers Grove, Ill.: InterVarsity Press, 1973), 41-42.

¹³⁹ See Mark 16:9.

¹⁴⁰ Matthew 6:5-6.

¹⁴¹ Matthew 26:37.

¹⁴² John 5:18; 7:1.

¹⁴³ Matthew 27:50; Mark 15:37; Luke 23:46; John 19:30-37.

¹⁴⁴ See Matthew 26:4; Mark 9:31; 10:34; Luke 22:2; John 5:18; 7:1.

¹⁴⁵ New Living Translation.

¹⁴⁶ New International Version.

[147] Revised Standard Version; New Revised Standard Version.

[148] These numbers follow Robert G. Bratcher, *Old Testament Quotations in the New Testament* (New York: United Bible Societies, 1984), 81-88.

[149] For a thorough treatment of the relationship between Hosea 11:1 and Matthew 2:15, see John H. Sailhamer, "Hosea 11:1 and Matthew 2:15," *Westminster Theological Journal* 63 (2001): 87-96.

[150] Numbers 23:7, 18; 24:3, 15, 20, 21, 23.

[151] Numbers 24:17.

[152] See John H. Sailhamer, "The Canonical Approach to the OT: Its Effect On Understanding Prophecy," *Journal of the Evangelical Theological Society* 30/3 (September 1987): 307-315.

[153] Mark 16:16; Acts 2:38; 8:16; 10:46-48; 19:1-6.

[154] Deuteronomy 18:15-19.

[155] II Peter 3:18.

NOTES

NOTES

NOTES

NOTES